Think RE!

Michael Brewer • Ruth Mantin

Peter Smith • Cavan Wood

Series editor: Janet Dyson Consultant: Pamela Draycott

www.heinemann.co.uk
✓ Free online support
✓ Useful weblinks
✓ 24 hour online ordering

01865 888058

Heinemann
Inspiring generations

Heinemann is an imprint of Pearson Education Limited, a company incorporated in England and Wales, having its registered office at Edinburgh Gate, Harlow, Essex, CM20 2JE.
Registered company number: 872828

Heinemann is a registered trademark of
Pearson Education Limited

First published 2005

09 08
10 9 8 7 6

British Library Cataloguing in Publication Data is available
from the British Library on request.

ISBN: 978 0 435307 26 4

Designed by Bridge Creative Services Ltd

Original illustrations © Harcourt Education Limited, 2005
Illustrated by Jane Smith and Andrew Skilleter

Printed and bound in China (EPC/06)

Cover photo © Corbis

Picture research by Bea Ray

Acknowledgements

Every effort has been made to contact copyright holders of material reproduced in this book. Any omissions will be rectified in subsequent printings if notice is given to the publishers.

Faith readers

Thanks to the following for advice on all the religious content:

Jonathan Brandman   Board of Deputies of British Jews
Rasamandala Das   Oxford Centre for Vishnu Hindu Studies
Anil Goonewardene   Buddhist Society
Dick Powell   Culham Institute
Professor Ghulam Sarwar   Muslim Educational Trust
Bhupinder Singh   United Sikhs

Copyright material

The author and publisher would like to thank the following for permission to use copyright material:
p. 43 Jubilee Campaign image © Jubilee Campaign; p. 49 Traidcraft logo and text © Traidcraft;
p. 51 Tearfund text © Tearfund; p. 58 Newspaper article © *Daily Telegraph*, 5 June 2004 .

Photo acknowledgements

The author and publisher would like to thank the following for permission to use photographs:
pp. 4, 5, 6, 7, 11, 16, 18, 19, 23, 28, 29, 30, 34 Getty; pp. 10, 12, 17, 21 (top, middle and bottom), 25, 27, 31, 37 (left, middle and right), 38, 39 (top and bottom), 40, 48 (right), 52, 54, 55 (right and left), 68, 75, 77, 88, 91, 93 (foreground), 95, 96, 97, 102, 103, 104, 108 Corbis; pp. 13, 32 (top and bottom), 60, 63, 67 (bottom), 76, 82, Rex Features; p. 26 Camera Press; p. 33 Leeds Postcards/Margaret Pauffley; p. 35 AP; p. 41 Gina Glover; pp. 46, 47 Pingalwara www.pingalwaraonline.org; pp. 48 (left), 49, 106 Alamy; p. 51 Mike Holloway/Tearfund; p. 58 Telegraph Group Ltd/David Howells; p. 59 Getty/Hulton/Fox; pp. 61, 65, 79, 83, Bridgeman Art Library; p. 62 Getty/Time Life; p. 67 (top) Quaker Society; p. 69 Reuters/Ian Waldie; pp. 70, 71 Tibet images; p. 78 Reuters; pp. 93 (background) 94, 109 Getty images/PhotoDisc; p. 100 Alamy/David Hoffman; p. 105 Panos Pictures/Rod Johnson; p. 107 Steve Rohrbach.

CR
20.7
THI

CONTENTS

PUTTING BELIEF AND FAITH INTO PRACTICE

THE BIGGER PICTURE

In this chapter you will investigate the difference between belief and faith. You will study two areas in which they affect the actions of religious believers: worship and the treatment of other people.

WHAT?

You will:

- investigate worship, including hero worship
- understand how religion inspires people
- explore how religion influences people in the way they treat others
- investigate how two organizations help people in need.

HOW?

By:

- learning about worship in two religions
- identifying important features of worship
- evaluating the practices of these religions
- reflecting on your own experiences.

WHY?

Because:

- the actions of religious believers affect everybody
- for many people, worship is a natural and understandable human response to something or someone that fills them with wonder
- many people rely on the actions of religious believers to help and support them.

A Buddhist meditating.

KEY IDEAS

- Faith leads to action.
- All religions include prayer, meditation or worship as part of their religious practice.
- Religious people believe that their religion should influence the way they behave.
- The need to look after other people is a central belief in all religions.
- Some religious people become involved in organizations that help those in need.

KEY WORDS

Worship	Priest
Idols	Murtis
Prayers	Church
Denomination	Quakers
Pentecostal	Praise
Congregation	Absolution
Transubstantiation	Salah
Mosque	Submission
Fellowship	Wudu
Imam	Paradise
Halal	Haram
Shahadah	Zakah

Muslims praying.

In this lesson you will:
- use evidence to help you decide whether certain actions could be described as worship
- examine what is meant by 'hero worship'
- investigate the role of religious worship for individuals and communities.

Worship is nothing new. Thousands of years ago, people would worship their leaders, the sun and planets, even their ancestors – anything they thought was great or that **inspired** awe and wonder. They often thought of these things or people as gods.

This worship took various forms:
- people would pray, sing, chant and dance
- they might have offered **sacrifices** – killing animals or even humans as the climax of some worship
- others offered crops and fruit rather than lives
- usually a **priest**, who had great power over people, led their worship.

Nowadays, worship is a little different, although many of the principles behind it remain the same.

Look at the photo on this page. It is of an Aztec/Mayan temple in Mexico. The Aztecs worshipped hundreds of gods. They believed that each god was in charge of a human activity or an aspect of nature. They built temples like the one in the picture to worship and make offerings to their gods.

● HERO WORSHIP

Can you think of someone you admire? How do you show this person respect?

Some people admire famous people so much that they almost seem to worship them. They might have pictures of them on their wall and collect information about them. They might join a fan club to meet other people who feel the same way. Or they might communicate with other fans on the Internet or by email. Some people would call this 'hero worship'.

Sometimes these heroes are referred to as **idols**. 'Idol' means a respected person or a god. Many religions do not like to use the word 'idol' to refer to images of their god. However, does this mean that the famous musicians and footballers we describe as idols can or should be seen as gods?

🎧 **Mayan pyramid at Chichen Itza, Yucatan, Mexico.**

Some people can be inspired by special objects. A piece of art, architecture, or even a piece of memorabilia connected with a hero or idol might prompt the desire to worship it. Is this really worship or simply special treatment? What do you think?

As a Hindu, I use statues of deities to focus my worship. I call them **murtis** and do not see them as idols.

Maya

? THINK ABOUT IT!

1. Explain in your own words what you think the word 'worship' means.

2. Give an example of one person and one object that might inspire people to worship. Explain how and why this might happen.

● RELIGIOUS WORSHIP

Some people are inspired by their beliefs to worship God. They believe that they can express their love of God through worship. This worship can take place either individually or with other people (public worship). Worship can give believers a sense of belonging, an identity, and encourages them to live their life in a way that they think pleases God.

Public worship is often led by a person respected by the believers. These leaders might say **prayers**, pass on advice to believers and read from sacred writings, for example the Bible or the Qur'an, to spread the teachings of the religion. You will learn more about what happens in Christian and Muslim worship later in this chapter.

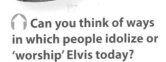
Can you think of ways in which people idolize or 'worship' Elvis today?

? THINK ABOUT IT!

3. **a)** Copy and complete the table below. Use the information on these pages and your own ideas. You can add to this table as you go through the chapter.

   b) Using the information from your table, say whether or not you think religious worship is different from hero worship. Explain your opinion.

Features of hero worship	Features of religious worship

1.2 WHERE DO CHRISTIANS WORSHIP?

In this lesson you will:
- explore the symbolizm used in churches
- raise questions about the need for a special building for worship.

KEY WORDS

Church Building where Christians worship or the whole community of Christians

Denomination A branch of Christianity

Quakers Christian group, otherwise known as the Religious Society of Friends, which was established by George Fox in the 17th century and which advocates pacifism

● CHRISTIAN CHURCHES

Christians worship in different places. Public worship often takes place in a special building called a **church** (or a chapel for non-conformists). Churches tend to be located in the town centre giving them prominence within the community. Some churches are old and highly decorated, but others might be more modern or simpler inside. Whatever they look like, these buildings are believed to be important because they help to inspire worship.

The design of a church often reflects the beliefs of the **denomination** as well as encouraging worship. For example, in Catholic and Anglican churches the design reflects the beliefs surrounding Holy Communion so the altar is the focus. In non-conformist chapels, on the other hand, the Bible or the Word is the focus and so the pulpit is more prominent and is larger.

Some key features of a typical church

Altar or communion table: this is at the eastern end of the church and is often the focal point of worship. Holy Communion is received here.

Organ: provides accompaniment to the singing.

Pulpit: a raised platform where the priest will preach his sermon.

Pews: these are wooden benches on which worshippers sit.

Font: used for baptism, this is often near the door to symbolize that baptism marks entry into the Christian Church.

Stained glass windows: these are made of coloured glass and often tell a story. This was useful hundreds of years ago when most people could not read.

Choir stalls: seats for the choir who lead singing during worship.

Lectern: where the Bible is read. It is often made of brass and in the shape of an eagle. This symbolizes the Word of God being spread worldwide.

Confessional: this is found in Roman Catholic and some Anglican churches. This is a place where people can confess their sins to a priest and receive forgiveness.

Many **Roman Catholic** churches and some **Anglican** churches are highly decorated and ornate. However, denominations like the **Baptists** and the **Methodists** tend to have churches that are designed more simply, but they still have most of the features shown on the page opposite. Great care is taken to ensure they are designed and maintained to inspire worship amongst believers.

THINK ABOUT IT!

1. **a)** Choose which of the features of a church shown in the image on page 8 you feel is the most important. Say why you think it is the most important.
   b) Now do the same with the feature you feel is the least important. Explain your choice.

● ALTERNATIVES TO CHURCHES

A special building is not essential for worship.
- Some groups meet for worship in people's houses.
- Others might worship in larger public buildings such as leisure centres.
- One group called the Ecclesia (the people of God) worship in schools.
- Some might worship in the open air.
- **Quakers** worship in a plain, simple room called a 'meeting house'. The only furniture they have are chairs for worshippers to sit on and a table at the front or in the centre. These people believe that where they worship is less important than the fact that they are coming together to worship.

● ARE CHURCHES ONLY USED FOR WORSHIP?

Many churches, whether old or new, have a separate building for use within the local community. This is usually called a church hall or parish hall.
- Youth and community groups often use it for meetings or activities, for example mother and toddler groups.
- Christians might use the hall to celebrate festivals. They might have a Christmas dinner or hold a nativity play in the build-up to Christmas to help believers to focus on the meaning of Christmas.
- Churches might also hold concerts where musicians or singers perform special religious pieces of music. Some people might regard this as a type of worship, with the music inspiring them to think of the greatness of God.

I like to worship in a beautiful church because, although it is very expensive to keep it looking nice, I think only the best is good enough for God.

It is not important to me where I worship; what is important is that I am fulfilling my duty to God.

THINK ABOUT IT!

2. Why do you think many Christians prefer to worship in a special building (church)?

3. Comment on what the people in the cartoons are saying. Who do you agree with and why?

4. 'Christians should spend less money on churches.' With a partner, think of some questions you could ask a person who believes this statement to be true. How might they answer your questions?

In this lesson you will:
- gain knowledge and understanding of Christian worship especially Holy Communion
- identify the key features of Christian worship
- evaluate the importance for Christians of coming together to worship.

KEY WORDS

Pentecostal A group of Christians who focus on praising God in worship

Praise To express positive feelings for God

Congregation Collection of people who worship in church

Absolution God's forgiveness passed on by a priest

Transubstantiation Belief that bread and wine actually turn into Jesus' body and blood

Christians agree that one way of showing how their beliefs influence their actions is in their worship of God. However, what form the worship should take varies from denomination to denomination. Some Christians may worship on their own, but most prefer to worship with other Christians. Meeting other Christians provides support in their beliefs and the opportunity to learn more about the Christian faith.

Some groups, for example Quakers (Society of Friends), have long periods of silent reflection in their worship. They feel this gives them a greater spiritual experience and a greater awareness of the presence of God. Others, such as **Pentecostal** Christians, have lots of singing and sometimes dancing. They emphasize the **praise** side of worship, letting God know how much they love him.

THINK ABOUT IT!

1. a) Talk to your partner about things you prefer to do on your own and things you prefer to do in a group. Explain why in each instance.
   b) Explain at least one reason why a Christian may prefer to worship alone and at least one reason why they may want to worship with others.

KEY FEATURES OF PUBLIC WORSHIP

- Led by a priest, vicar or minister
- A talk (sermon) – this might explain one of the readings
- Prayer – communicating with, giving thanks and expressing love for God
- A chance to give money to fund the work of the church
- Music – hymns, psalms and other religious songs are often sung, praising God
- **Key features of Christian worship**
- Meeting other Christians and sharing experiences (fellowship)
- Holy Communion – a service during which Christians share bread and wine together in memory of Jesus
- Readings – taken from the Bible
- Usually takes place in a church

WHAT IS HOLY COMMUNION?

Most Christian churches hold a special service called Holy Communion. Holy Communion can also be called Eucharist, Thanksgiving, Mass or the Lord's Supper.

- Roman Catholics often hold this service every day and call it Mass.
- Other denominations, for example Methodists, might hold Holy Communion once a month.
- In the Church of England, it usually happens every Sunday.

The actual Holy Communion service is usually quite short. It can be a part of the regular Sunday worship. If so, it will follow on from some of the activities above like singing hymns, Bible readings and the sermon. It can also be celebrated on its own.

Holy Communion is based on the Last Supper Jesus had with his disciples just before he was arrested. At the Last Supper, Jesus gave bread and wine to his disciples. He told them the bread was his body and the wine was his blood, and that they should continue to share bread and wine with each other once he was dead. He wanted them to do this in order to remember him.

WHAT HAPPENS DURING HOLY COMMUNION IN AN ANGLICAN CHURCH?

- The priest or vicar will say prayers on behalf of the **congregation**. Some will be said together, including a prayer where the congregation confesses their sins to God.
- The priest will give them **absolution** or forgiveness from God.
- He will then offer more prayers including one that reminds the congregation of the Last Supper.
- He blesses the bread and wine, which has already been brought to the altar.
- The congregation will then walk towards the altar, kneel and receive a small piece of bread (or small wafer) from a plate called a paten and a sip of wine (often mixed with holy water) from a cup called a chalice.

WHAT DO PEOPLE BELIEVE ABOUT HOLY COMMUNION?

- Roman Catholics believe that the bread and wine actually turn into Jesus' body and blood when taken into the mouth. They call this **transubstantiation**.
- Most Protestants, for example Anglicans or Methodists, believe the bread and wine represent Jesus' body and blood.
- In taking Holy Communion, Christians feel they are obeying Jesus' instruction to his disciples.

Methodists are not encouraged to drink alcohol. Therefore they will have non-alcoholic red fruit juice, which they drink from small individual glasses. This is one way in which their beliefs influence their actions even in such an important act of worship.

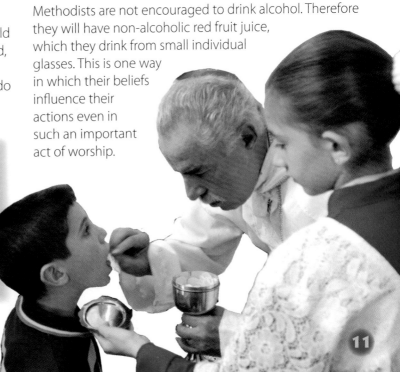

Pentecostal Christians worshipping.

Christians taking Holy Communion.

11

In this lesson you will:
- explore key features of Muslim worship
- evaluate the requirement to pray five times a day
- investigate ideas associated with preparation for prayer
- compare the key features of Muslim and Christian worship.

KEY WORDS

Salah One of the five pillars instructing Muslims to pray to Allah five times a day

Mosque Building where Muslims worship

Submission Giving into the will of God or another person

Fellowship Community within a religion

Wudu Muslim practice of washing before prayer

Imam A leader of prayer in Islam

Imagine being expected to do a particular thing at exactly the same time every day. You would probably find it difficult, especially if you are already doing something else at that time. Muslims are expected to pray five times every day.

SALAH

The second pillar of Islam is **salah**. Salah means prayer five times every day. The times of prayer vary with the times of sunrise and sunset. However, two prayer times are during the hours of darkness and three during the day.

When Muslims hear the call to prayer from the **mosque**, they should stop what they are doing and begin their prayers. If they are too far from a mosque to hear the call to prayer, they have to rely on a timetable.

Muslims believe that prayer five times a day is an important way of showing their obedience and **submission** to Allah. It also emphasizes their **fellowship** with Muslims around the world.

⏪ **Muslims praying in a Mosque in Yugoslavia.**

THINK ABOUT IT!

1. Write down and explain one advantage and one disadvantage of having to pray five times a day. Once you have done this, discuss your ideas with your partner and add their ideas to your own.

● WORSHIP IN THE MOSQUE

The mosque is open all week. However, the main time for worship is Friday lunchtime. When they hear the call to prayer, all Muslim men are required to go to the mosque for communal worship. Women are allowed to choose whether they go or not, but they should still say prayers.

Before they enter the prayer hall in the mosque, Muslims are required to remove their shoes and perform **wudu**. This means they have to wash certain parts of the body with water. They do this in the same way every time to make sure they are prepared to stand before Allah.

They start with their right hand, then their left, finishing with their left foot and ankle. Having washed their mouth, face and arms they wipe their heads with wet hands and run their wet fingers through the grooves of their ears.

? THINK ABOUT IT!

2. What do you think is significant about the use of water in religion?

3. Explain why you think Muslims believe it is important to wash before prayer.

Once wudu is finished, Muslims will make their way into their prayer hall. Men and women pray separately, either in different rooms or in different parts of the same hall. If a family has very young children, they usually pray at home with their mother whilst their father is in the mosque. Older children will go to the mosque.

During the Friday prayers, the **imam** (leader of the prayer) will preach a sermon explaining a portion of the Qur'an or giving advice on what it means to be a Muslim.

Sabeel

> I enjoy going to the mosque. It means I can pray with all my Muslim friends and learn more about Allah at the same time.

Muslims performing wudu.

? THINK ABOUT IT!

4. a) Complete the table on features of worship that you began earlier in the chapter.

b) Once you have filled in the features of Christian and Muslim worship, prepare a short Powerpoint presentation using bullet points to explain what you think are the main similarities and differences in the way the two religions worship.

1.5 DOES BELIEF AFFECT DAILY LIFE?

In this lesson you will:
- explain the impact of religious rules on the lives of Muslims
- explore the difficulties involved in living by some religious rules
- consider the impact of rules in your own life.

WHERE DO RELIGIOUS PEOPLE GO FOR GUIDANCE?

Many people live happy and successful lives, deciding for themselves what to do. However, they might look for guidance in difficult situations. For religious people, this guidance often comes from their religious beliefs and can be built into their normal way of life.

Islam has clear rules about many aspects of life. Muslims believe that these rules help them deal with all situations and problems in life.

MUSLIM RULES ABOUT ALCOHOL

> 'Strong drink…is part of Satan's [the devil's] handiwork. Leave it aside in order that you may succeed.'
>
> *Qur'an 5: 90*

The Qur'an forbids Muslims to drink alcohol. They believe that they must never have their mind clouded by alcohol (or other drugs) because if they do, they cannot focus on Allah or serve him properly. This might prevent them from going to **paradise** with Allah when they die.

THINK ABOUT IT!

1. **a)** If you had a problem in school that you felt you needed advice about, where would you look to find this advice? Explain why.
   b) What if the problem was to do with your family or a friend? Where would you go? Who would you ask?

THINK ABOUT IT!

2. In pairs have a debate about the Qur'an quotation given above. The first person should argue for 2 minutes in defence of the quotation and the second person should argue for 2 minute against it. Who had the most persuasive argument?

Go on. No one will know. If it wasn't ok they wouldn't sell it.

No thanks. It's wrong and Allah will know if I do.

● WHAT ABOUT FOOD?

As well as having rules about alcohol, Muslims also have rules about the types of food they can eat. The food they can eat is called **halal**. The food they cannot eat is called **haram**.

- All animals must be killed with as little pain and cruelty as possible, but the animal must be conscious.
- The **Shahadah** is said whilst the animal is killed with a sharp knife. The blood is then washed from the meat.

- Animals that only eat grass such as cows and sheep are halal. Nothing from the pig is allowed.
- Fish must have fins and scales to be halal, so shellfish are haram.
- Birds that do not scavenge on other creatures are halal, for example chicken and turkey.
- Dairy products, fruit and vegetables are all halal.

HALAL FOOD

The spider diagram above shows the food which Muslims can eat (halal). Can you draw a similar diagram for the food they can't eat (haram)?

THINK ABOUT IT!

3. Write a menu for a three-course meal that would be suitable for a Muslim. Ask your partner whether he or she thinks you are correct.

● IS IT ALWAYS EASY?

Not all rules are as straightforward to follow as the rules about food and alcohol. Sometimes rules are more difficult to interpret, for example 'Do not kill anyone' (Qur'an, Surah 17: 33). Most religious people would agree that this is a good rule because it makes murder completely wrong. However, how can this rule be applied to war, self-defence or capital punishment?

THINK ABOUT IT!

4. **a)** Explain what you think 'Do not kill' means.
   b) What difficulties might this rule present to a religious believer?

5. What is the hardest rule for you to keep in your own life?

In this lesson you will:
- explore the link between faith and relief work
- identify religious and non-religious reasons for helping people in need
- justify providing help for people in need.

KEY WORDS
Zakah Islamic practice of giving 2.5 per cent of savings to those in need

THE LINK BETWEEN BELIEF AND ACTION

Many religious people believe that their faith is meaningless if it does not make a difference to what they do. They cannot sit back knowing that people are suffering and that they are doing nothing to help. Humanists are also keen to help people in need, purely because they believe this is the right thing to do.

Although religious people help those in need as part of their religion, they might also do so because it is a basic human responsibility.

Tsunami – a worldwide response

On 26 December 2004, an earthquake measuring 8.9 on the Richter scale occurred around 60 miles off the coast of Indonesia. This triggered huge tidal waves called tsunami, which devastated coastal areas up to 3700 miles away. The destruction was enormous and over 225,000 people were killed. Most of these people lived in the affected areas, but thousands of foreign holidaymakers also lost their lives.

WHAT CAN BE DONE TO HELP?

Once the rest of the world heard about the tragedy, a massive relief operation was launched. In Britain, this was co-ordinated by the Disasters Emergency Committee (DEC). This is a group of charities set up in 1963 to co-ordinate relief work on behalf of many charities. Some of these are Christian organizations such as Christian Aid and CAFOD, whilst others like Oxfam and Save the Children have no specific religious motivation.

Religious or not, it did not seem to matter, as people in Britain raised over £250 million to fund relief work. In Britain and throughout the world, people of all religions and non-religious people alike have been keen to help.

> 'Whatever you did for one of the least of these brothers of mine, you did for me…whatever you did not do for one of the least of these, you did not do for me.'
>
> *Matthew 25: 40, 45*

Earthquake – an Islamic response

On 26 December 2003, an earthquake measuring 6.3 on the Richter scale hit the city of Bam in South East Iran. Over half of the buildings in Bam were completely destroyed. This included thousands of homes.

Immediately, the Iranian Red Crescent, an Islamic **charity**, sent 500 rescuers and relief workers, together with medical teams to the area. They took with them mobile hospitals, ambulances, tents, blankets, food and water. Over the next few days, they sent many more people, most of them with medical skills, to help the people of Bam. Vast amounts of food, water, clothing and equipment to help with the rescue efforts were also provided by the Iranian Red Crescent, assisted financially by relief organizations throughout the world.

It is estimated that around 30,000 people were killed in the earthquake. Many thousands of survivors needed emergency medical treatment. The food distribution programme, organized by the Iranian Red Crescent, helped 220,000 people. 160,000 still needed help ten weeks after the earthquake.

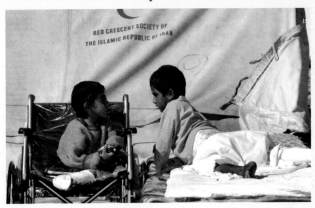

‘Righteous is he who gives his wealth, for the love of Allah, to relatives, orphans, the needy and the traveller, and those who ask for help...’

Qur'an 2: 177

For the Muslims involved with the Red Crescent, giving a small amount of charity (**zakah**) every year is not enough. They feel they have to do something more to help. They believe that if they are helping, they are doing their duty to their fellow Muslims and also to Allah.

THINK ABOUT IT!

1. Design a leaflet to promote the work of the DEC in response to the tsunami disaster or the work of the Red Crescent in Iran. You need to include:
    *   information about the problem
    *   information about what the DEC or the Red Crescent have done to help
    *   an explanation of why people are keen to support the DEC and the Red Crescent
    *   suggestions about what further help you think may be needed
    *   ideas about why the DEC or the Red Crescent believe they have a duty to help.

    You can find out more information from their websites by visiting www.heinemann.co.uk/hotlinks, typing in the express code 7266P and clicking on this section.

2. Imagine you are trying to organise a fundraising event to help victims of the Tsunami. Someone in your class says, 'I don't see why we should bother to help, it's nothing to do with us'. How would you respond?

WHAT THE TASK IS ALL ABOUT:

Choose one of the following tasks:

1. Produce a small book to be used with pupils in Years 3 and 4 in their RE lessons to help them to:
   - understand why being religious involves taking action
   - learn how people in at least one religion worship
   - make links with the things and people who influence their own lives.

   Make the book by taking a piece A4 paper, folding it in four and cutting the top edges.

2. Write a letter to a friend. In your letter you should tell them what you have learnt in this chapter.
   - Explain how religion affects a believer's day-to-day life in obeying rules and helping others.
   - Express your own ideas about how a religious person should behave towards other people.
   - Refer to any similarities and differences between religions.
   - Make links with your own religious or non-religious experiences.

WHAT YOU NEED TO DO TO COMPLETE THE TASK:

- You will need to sort out your ideas and decide what information is relevant before you start writing.
- Think carefully about what belief and faith are and then link them to people's actions.
- Make sure you think either about worship or how religion affects people's lives.
- You will need to give your own ideas as well, so do not forget to work out your reasons for your opinion.
- You can choose to focus on just one religion or compare two if you prefer.
- Once you have sorted out all your information, you can decide how to set it out in your letter or booklet.
- You may want to include some simple pictures to illustrate your booklet.

HINTS AND TIPS

- Make sure you include enough detail to answer your question in full.
- When you give your opinion, you should give your reasons as well.
- Once you have given your reasons, try to think of a different opinion from your own and give reasons for that different opinion as well.
- Try to show how their religious beliefs affect what a person thinks or does.
- Make the links between belief, faith and action clear and show how the actions affect people.
- In both tasks you need to think of your audience and write in a way that will help your friend or the children to understand.

TO ACHIEVE	YOU WILL NEED TO
Level 3	Use the correct words to describe some religious beliefs and actions. Show that you understand the importance of religious beliefs and teachings in helping people decide how to behave and worship.
Level 4	Describe how people worship and/or act in at least one religion, referring to any similarities and differences. Describe how religious belief affects people's lives. Show that you understand the experiences of religious people and use your own experience and ideas to show why they do what they do. Describe what influences your own life.
Level 5	Explain why people belong to religions and how religious beliefs and teachings make a difference to people's lives and the life of the community. Identify some similarities and differences in worship and behaviour between the religions you have studied. Make links with your own experiences and give your views on the challenges of belonging to a religion.
Level 6	Write a detailed account of how belief affects the way people behave in two religions, explaining the reasons for similarities and differences between them. Explain your own and other people's views about what it means to belong to a religion or other group and what might make commitment difficult for some people today.

PREJUDICE

THE BIGGER PICTURE

In this unit you will explore key teachings in religious traditions about prejudice and, in particular, racism. You will discover how different people have challenged racism. You will be encouraged to understand why racism develops and to reflect on your own ideas.

WHAT?

You will:
- understand key terms such as prejudice, racism and discrimination
- explore how followers of Christianity (Martin Luther King), Hinduism (Mahatma Gandhi) and Islam (Malcolm X) have responded to racism and how their faith inspired their actions
- make links between beliefs, behaviour and prejudice
- investigate the ways in which people respond to racist behaviour
- reflect on whether or not religion adds to or reduces prejudice.

HOW?

By:
- reflecting on your own ideas about prejudice
- looking at the causes of prejudice and racism
- studying the life and work of Gandhi
- comparing and contrasting the life and work of Martin Luther King and Malcolm X
- examining the teachings of Christianity, Islam and Hinduism with regard to racism
- exploring whether religion helps solve or contributes to the issue of prejudice.

WHY?

Because:
- we need to understand what it means to be part of a multi-cultural society and how religious and non-religious responses can help in supporting tolerance and acceptance between people
- it is important to understand how racism develops as a result of factors such as wealth, history, religion, culture, fear and lack of knowledge.

Martin Luther King speaks to a crowd at the 'March Against Fear' rally on the steps of Mississippi State Capitol.

KEY IDEAS

- Prejudice and discrimination can be found in many aspects of life and have existed throughout history.
- There are many different types of discrimination.
- Many people believe in responding to prejudice with non-violence – not hitting back but using peaceful means to protest.
- Ahimsa is the Hindu concept of not harming any living thing.
- Civil rights campaigners in the USA aimed to secure equal rights for black people in terms of schooling, voting, jobs and services.

Malcolm X addresses a rally in Harlem on 14 May 1963 in support of desegregation in Birmingham, Alabama.

KEY WORDS

Stereotyping	Prejudice
Discrimination	Racism
Scapegoating	Ashram
Ahimsa	Brahman
Castes	Untouchables
Segregation	Hadith

Mahatma Gandhi at 10 Downing Street, 1931.

In this lesson you will:
- understand the meaning of key words connected with prejudice and how to use them correctly
- reflect on reasons why people show prejudice and discrimination.

KEY WORDS

Stereotyping A generalised and simplistic mental idea of a group which is usually negative

Prejudice Believing some people are inferior or superior without even knowing them

Discrimination To act on the basis of prejudice

Racism The belief that some races are superior to others

Scapegoating To blame things that go wrong on a particular person or group

'The Holocaust did not start with a concentration camp. It started with a brick through the shop window of a Jewish business...and the shout of racist abuse on the street.'

Tony Blair, Holocaust Memorial Day, 2005

THINK ABOUT IT!

1. How do you think the quotation above is relevant today?

WE ARE ALL ONE?

People are often divided into groups, either by themselves or by others. They might be divided by:

- age – young, middle-aged and elderly
- gender – male and female
- class – working, middle and upper
- where they live
- what football team they follow
- the colour of their skin
- family
- ethnic background

Grouping people like this can lead to **stereotyping**. Stereotyping is when particular characteristics are linked to a certain group. For example, you could say that all young people are rude and all elderly people are grumpy!

WHAT IS PREJUDICE?

It is not necessarily wrong to group people. What is wrong is pre-judging people based on which group they belong to. This can lead to **prejudice**.

Prejudice is when people form opinions about another person or group. The word 'prejudice' usually suggests that these opinions are negative. Prejudice can be caused by a number of different factors.

- Ignorance: prejudice can be the result of not understanding why other people do or think certain things.

- Fear: some people might feel that a particular group presents a threat to their way of life or to their jobs or opportunities.
- Some prejudice is learnt behaviour: parents, for example, might influence the attitudes of their children.
- It might be the result of an unfortunate experience one person had involving another group or individual.

WHAT IS DISCRIMINATION?

When prejudice leads someone to act against another person or group, then it becomes **discrimination**. To discriminate is to act on a particular prejudice, either for or against the group or individual.

Discrimination against people with a disability	Racism (discrimination against people because of their race)	Sexism (discrimination by gender)
Islamaphobia (discrimination against Muslims)	**Types of discrimination**	Ageism (discrimination due to age)
Xenophobia (discrimination against foreigners)	Anti-Semitism (discrimination against Jews)	Homophobia (discrimination against gay and lesbian people)

Jewish children in a Nazi concentration camp at Auschwitz – victims of anti-Semitism.

SCAPEGOATING

The Ancient Israelites believed that their relationship with God was tainted by their sins. They developed a system whereby a priest would recite all the sins of the people over a goat, which would then be driven off into the desert to die. This goat became known as the 'scapegoat'. The Israelites felt they had been cleansed of their sins by its death. This is where the term '**scapegoating**' originated.

Sometimes prejudice and discrimination can result in scapegoating. Nowadays, scapegoating means that the problems of one group are blamed on another. For example, in Nazi Germany, Jews were blamed for all the political and economic problems that Germany faced in the aftermath of the First World War. In history lessons, German teachers had to teach children that the Jews had wronged Germany throughout the centuries. This scapegoating led to a dramatic rise in discrimination against Jews, which eventually resulted in the **Holocaust**. Jewish people and other supposed enemies of the state, including homosexuals, gypsies and disabled people, were murdered in concentration camps during Hitler's reign.

THINK ABOUT IT!

2. What prejudices do you think you have?

3. In pairs, write definitions of 'discrimination', 'sexism', 'anti-Semitism' and 'Islamaphobia'. Agree a class definition for each term.

4. Who do you think are the modern-day scapegoats in the UK? Explain your answer.

5. Why do you think people are prejudiced? Are they born prejudiced or do they become prejudiced?

6. How do you think prejudice can be overcome? List five things people could do to stop prejudice developing.

2.2 WHO WAS GANDHI?

In this lesson you will:
- investigate how Gandhi reacted to racism
- explore Gandhi's belief in non-violence and his response to racism
- express your own views about how easy it would be to live in an ashram

KEY WORDS

Ashram An Indian word meaning 'spiritual community'

Ahimsa Non-violence, respect for life

Atman The Hindu belief in the soul, which is part of every living being

Brahman Eternal spirit which is different from temporary matter. It is the source of life in all living things and in the universe

THE 'GREAT SOUL'

Mohatma Gandhi was born in India in 1869 to a relatively wealthy Hindu family. He was called Mohandas, but later came to be known as Mahatma, which means 'great soul'. After training as a lawyer in London, he went to work in South Africa in 1890.

> I did not realize the extent of racism in South Africa. When I was on a train, a white customer complained to the guard that I was sitting in first class. Apparently, Indians are not allowed to sit here. The guard asked me to leave the compartment, but I refused – I had paid for a first class ticket and I had every right to sit there. The guard warned me that if I did not move, he would get the police and have me thrown off the train at the next station. I still refused to move, and at the next station, they threw me off.

The experience on the train encouraged Gandhi to help in the fight for basic respect and rights for the Indian community in South Africa. He objected to the fact that the South African government made Indians and blacks carry a document called a pass, unlike white people. If they did not have the pass on them, they could be fined or sent to prison.

Gandhi also protested against the way South African law made only Christian marriages legal, and against the appalling conditions many Indian workers faced in the mines.

THINK ABOUT IT!

1. How would you have reacted if you had been treated as Gandhi was on the train? Give reasons for your answer.

THE ASHRAM

One of the ways Gandhi drew attention to the racism he saw in South Africa was to set up an **ashram**. Ashram is an Indian word meaning 'spiritual community'. In Gandhi's ashram people of different religions, races and backgrounds shared all their possessions, ate together and were involved in the struggle for human rights. By bringing different people together to live in harmony, Gandhi hoped to show South Africa how evil racism was.

THINK ABOUT IT!

2. What problems do you think there might have been in the ashram? How do you think they could have been overcome? Give reasons for your answers.

When he returned to India, Gandhi again set up an ashram to show how different people could work together. He also aimed to challenge the rule of the British. Unity was important to Gandhi both as a way of life and in the struggle for independence. He felt he had learnt from all the different religions and all the people he had encountered.

● WHAT DID GANDHI BELIEVE?

As a Hindu, Gandhi was guided by a number of key ideas.

- **Ahimsa** – no harm should be done to any living thing.
- The belief that violence could never solve any problem. Using non-violence showed that Gandhi and his followers valued others and were prepared to suffer pain for their cause.
- Satya and satyagraha – meaning 'truth' and 'firmness in truth'. Gandhi believed that people should stick firmly to religious principles, and apply them in everyday life.
- Gandhi taught that people should try to be more humble and live more simply. He tried to live as simple a lifestyle as he could and thought a village lifestyle was the best.

By practising humility and non-violence, Gandhi believed that he could achieve inner peace and understand his real self. The real self (called the **atman**) is not the temporary body made of matter, but is made of **Brahman** (eternal spirit).

THINK ABOUT IT!

3. Gandhi once said, 'An eye for an eye and a tooth for a tooth would make the world blind and toothless.' Is Gandhi's idea that you should never seek revenge realistic? Give reasons for your answer, showing that you have thought about it from more than one point of view.

4. Working in pairs, use the information you have about Gandhi's ashram to develop a role-play about some of the problems that could arise when setting up an ashram.

   - One person should take on the role of someone who wants to set up an ashram.
   - The other person could be someone who has either previously lived in an ashram similar to Gandhi's or is thinking of living there.

Mohatma Gandhi in South Africa in c.1900. At this time he was a lawyer and wore Western clothes.

2.3 WHAT DID GANDHI DO IN INDIA?

In this lesson you will:
- evaluate how Gandhi's beliefs affected his work in India
- reflect on the impact of Gandhi in India and on the world today.

KEY WORDS

Varnas Four classes or groups that make up traditional Indian society

Jatis Sub-groups within a varna made up of numerous families who follow the same occupation (also known as castes)

Castes Sub-groups of people categorised according to the social group in which they are born (also known as Jatis)

Untouchables People who are seen as the lowest in the Hindu caste system

Imagine a funeral procession with around three million people, including the Prime Minister, taking part. This is the number of people who attended the funeral of Mohatma Gandhi in 1948. As you can see from the picture, he was a small, frail man. However, the influence he had on the people and government of India was enormous.

● GANDHI RETURNS TO INDIA

Traditionally, Indian society was based on a social system called varnashrama. This system divided people into four groups called **varnas**, with the priests and intellectuals at the top and manual workers at the bottom.

Over time, these four divisions have been further divided into thousands of sub-groups called **jatis**, or **castes** which were hereditary (based solely on birth). This complex social system is known by some as the caste system.

There also emerged a group called **untouchables** who are not members of any caste. These people do the most unpleasant jobs, such as cleaning.

When Gandhi returned to India in 1915, the country was still ruled by the British. This rule was called 'the Raj' or 'the British Raj', and it placed restrictions on what Indians could and could not do. British rule led to a decline in India's wealth, and made the caste system more rigid, highlighting the divide between the richest and poorest classes.

● WHAT DID GANDHI DO?

Although Gandhi was from a relatively wealthy family, he decided he must help the poor. Gandhi also wanted India to be free from British rule. He and his followers held marches and processions, demanding fairness for all people, but, as in South Africa, at no time did Gandhi allow the use of violence. Gandhi believed in ahimsa, non-violence.

Gandhi also believed that as a Hindu he should try to detach himself from the material things of this world. He gave up his wealth and often chose to live among the poor instead. He dreamt of an India in which Hindus and other religious communities lived side by side without prejudice or discrimination. People would live a simple, spiritual life in villages rather than in large towns and cities.

↑ **Mohatma Gandhi in simple Indian dress, 1931.**

?

THINK ABOUT IT!

1. **a)** Why do you think it was so important for Gandhi to go and live with the poor?
    b) What problems do you think he might have found?

Gandhi once said:

> 'My religion is Hinduism, which, for me, is the religion of humanity and includes the best of all religions known to me.'

Gandhi was able to see truth and insight in other religions. He once wrote that he had been particularly inspired by Jesus' teachings on non-violence in the Sermon on the Mount (Matthew 5–7) – Jesus tells his followers that they should turn the other cheek. Gandhi agreed with this because it calls for forgiveness and a non-violent response to racism and other injustices.

● INDEPENDENCE

Finally, in 1947, the British gave India independence (the chance to rule their own country). In 1948, a law was passed banning 'untouchability', which meant that people could no longer be discriminated against because of the family and the situation into which they were born. There were improvements to the life of some of India's poorest people, though to this day there are still many problems to be overcome.

Jawaharlal Nehru, the Indian Prime Minister at the time of Gandhi's death, said of him:

> 'The light that shone in this country was no ordinary light. It will light this country for many years and a thousand years later will still be seen.'

The funeral procession of Mohatma Gandhi in New Delhi, 8 February 1948.

THINK ABOUT IT!

2. In what ways do you think Gandhi was a light for the people of India? How might he be a light for people today? Give reasons for your answer.

3. Imagine you are a journalist interviewing Gandhi about his campaigns.
   a) Put together a list of questions that you would like to ask him about his life, work and beliefs.
   b) Based on your questions, write a newspaper article about Gandhi.

In this lesson you will:
- investigate the life and work of Martin Luther King
- explore the impact of Christianity on his life and teaching
- express your own ideas about what would make the world a better place.

KEY WORDS

Segregation Dividing people along racial, sexual or religious lines

How would you feel if one day your best friend was told by their mum that they could no longer visit you? How about if you saw your father mistreated and abused because of the colour of his skin?

These were just some of the things the American Christian leader Martin Luther King had experienced by his fifth birthday.

WHO WAS MARTIN LUTHER KING?

Martin Luther King was born in 1929 in Atlanta, Georgia, one of the southern states of the USA. He became a Christian minister, like his father.

At that time, many white people in the south of the USA did not treat black people as equals. Black people were not allowed to have good jobs. They could not mix freely with white people and they did not have the same rights as white people. They were treated little better than the slaves some of their ancestors had been. This system was called **segregation** because it separated blacks and whites. Segregation had developed following the end of slavery in the southern states of the USA.

A little black girl leaves a cafe through a door marked 'For coloured', c.1950. At this time people were divided by the colour of their skin.

WHAT DID MARTIN LUTHER KING BELIEVE?

During his lifetime, Martin Luther King faced prejudice because he was black. Some white people used the Bible to suggest that black people were created inferior to whites. For example, the story in Genesis 9 where Ham is given a blemish on his skin for disobeying God was used to say that black people were descendents of Ham.

King, however, taught that the real meaning of the Bible was to point out how important it was to treat all people with respect. King often talked about how people were children of God, made in God's image.

King also talked about the Parable of the Good Samaritan (Luke 10: 25–37). In this parable, Jesus made a racial enemy of Jewish people, a Samaritan, into the hero who helps a Jewish man in trouble. He did this so the Jews would understand that racial prejudice was wrong.

Above all, King was motivated by the Sermon on the Mount (Matthew 5–7), an important part of Jesus' teaching where Jesus encouraged his followers to love their enemies, to be selfless and not to seek revenge on those who had done them harm.

'You have heard that it was said, "Love your neighbour and hate your enemy." But I tell you: Love your enemies and pray for those who persecute you.'

Matthew 5: 43–4

● 'I HAVE A DREAM…'

Martin Luther King organized peaceful protest marches against the segregation of black and white people, involving as many as one million people, both black and white. Whenever a march took place, he delivered a speech. These speeches showed his great leadership qualities and his charisma. In August 1963, he made the best known of his speeches in which he stated:

> 'I have a dream that my four little children will one day live in a nation where they will not be judged by the colour of their skin but by the content of their character.'

Five years later, he was shot and killed as he stood on a hotel balcony. The police arrested a white man called James Earl Ray. Every January, Americans celebrate Martin Luther King Day to remember his achievements.

● ACHIEVEMENTS

By the time he died, Martin Luther King had helped achieve so much.
- There had been an end to discrimination on buses, in schools, parks and other public places.
- Black people had secured the right to vote.
- There were a number of black politicians at local and national level.
- It had become easier for black people to get jobs in the media, law, education and in business.

THINK ABOUT IT!

1. Read the Sermon on the Mount in Matthew 5–7. Which of its teachings do you think especially influenced Martin Luther King? Give reasons for your answer.

2. 'Love your enemies.' What do you think Jesus meant by this? Do you think this will ever be possible? Give reasons for your answer. How do you think Martin Luther King would respond to this?

THINK ABOUT IT!

3. Make a list of the key features of Martin Luther King's campaigns against segregation.

4. What might your dream of a better world include? Design a poster or write a poem to illustrate your ideas.

🎧 **Martin Luther King waves to the crowd of more than 200,000 people gathered on the Mall during the 'March on Washington' after delivering his 'I have a dream' speech, 28 August 1963.**

In this lesson you will:
- explore the life and work of Malcolm X
- reflect on your own experiences of having to say sorry and how it made you feel.
- investigate the contrasting beliefs that Malcolm X followed.

SAYING SORRY IS NEVER EASY

Think about a time when you have had to admit you are in the wrong. Was it difficult? It is likely that you would not want anyone to know about it. Sometimes we can get away with it without anybody knowing, but if you were a famous person, it would be much more difficult. Malcolm X faced having to make a public admission that he was wrong.

Malcolm X making a speech, 1963.

WHO WAS MALCOLM X?

Malcolm X was born Malcolm Little in Omaha, Nebraska, USA, on 19 May 1925. His father, Earl Little, was a black Baptist Christian. Malcolm had a troubled upbringing because many people did not like what his father preached. Malcolm's father challenged people to think about their racist behaviour.

At school Malcolm was the only black child in his class and he was very bright. When he was fourteen he decided he wanted to become a lawyer, but was told that this was unlikely to happen because he was black. Like his father he despised the racism of the whites and protested against their treatment of the blacks.

Two years later, he went to live with his sister in Boston. He became addicted to drugs, turned to crime and was sent to prison. During his time in prison, he followed the example of many young black men and became a Muslim. After meeting the leader of the Nation of Islam, Elijah Muhammad, Malcolm X had come to believe that Christianity was the religion that white people had used to make black people slaves. He also believed that Islam was the religion of his ancestors.

MALCOLM JOINS THE NATION OF ISLAM

After being released from prison in 1952, Malcolm joined a group called the Nation of Islam and changed his name from Malcolm Little to Malcolm X. This group were against integration between blacks and white. They wanted blacks to enjoy equal rights while remaining distinct and separate from whites. They were prepared to use violence to achieve this. Malcolm X made many speeches in support of this idea, which nowadays would be seen as racist. He did not want races to be equal; he wanted black people to have the power. He himself became a very powerful leader and was hated by many people.

THINK ABOUT IT!

1. Why do you think Malcolm X was attracted to the Nation of Islam?

MALCOLM GOES TO MAKKAH

In March 1964, Malcolm X went on a pilgrimage to Makkah and was amazed that all pilgrims were considered equal regardless of their colour. On this journey, he learnt that people could be treated equally, and he began to question his prejudices. He met fellow Muslims who were white and who treated him with respect. He realized his racist ideas were wrong and changed his way of thinking completely.

On 17 April 1964 he wrote in his diary:

> 'The crowds were of all colours, bowing in unison [together]…I was not conscious of colour for the first time in my life.'

Later, he described the change in his ideas and beliefs:

> 'Out of sudden darkness comes sudden light.'

THINK ABOUT IT!

2. Write a diary entry for Malcolm X describing the effect that the pilgrimage had on him. Include his thoughts on what he witnessed and how his views changed as a result.

3. At one point in his life, Malcolm X told black people that they should use 'any means necessary' to defend themselves against attack. Do you think that violence could help stop racism or will it always make it worse? Organize a class debate on this.

Muslim pilgrims pray at the Grand Mosque in Makkah, 17 January 2005. About 2 million Muslims gathered for their Hajj pilgrimage in 2005.

WHAT HAPPENED NEXT?

Following the pilgrimage, Malcolm X issued a public apology for his formerly racist views. He left the Nation of Islam and formed his own, non-racist organization. He set up mosques across the USA and also began to talk to Martin Luther King to plan campaigns to help with the fight against racism. The latter unfortunately made him a target for white racists. All of these actions were a sign that he was becoming increasingly aware of the unity of all peoples. As stated in the **Hadith**: 'He who eats and drinks while his brother goes hungry, is not one of us.'

On 21 February 1965, Malcolm X was shot dead in New York by three men, probably from the Nation of Islam, who felt that he had betrayed the movement.

THINK ABOUT IT!

4. a) Do you think it was easy or difficult for Malcolm X to say publicly he was wrong after he had experienced people living together in harmony when he went to Makkah?

   b) In your opinion, was he right to be open about his changed views? Give reasons for your answer, showing that you have thought about it from more than one point of view.

2.6 DOES RACISM STILL EXIST?

In this lesson you will:
- explore how Christians respond to racism
- identify the problems still to be overcome
- explain your own response to the issue of racism.

THE THREE STEPHENS

At the Greenbelt Christian festival in 1999, Robert Beckford, a black English theologian, said black Christians in the UK have three Stephens they should look to.

1 St Stephen
St Stephen was the first person to be killed by the Jewish authorities for standing up for his Christian beliefs. He was killed within a few years of Jesus, perhaps around 35CE.

THINK ABOUT IT!

1. Read the story of Stephen's martyrdom in Acts 7–8. Why do you think the black Christian community considers this an important story?

2 Steven Biko
Steven Biko was a black human rights campaigner in South Africa who urged blacks to think of how they could free themselves. He reminded them of the need to believe in themselves and not to be dictated to by the prejudices of the then white and racist South African government. Biko was arrested, tortured and killed by the South African police in 1977 for his outspoken attack on the evil of racism in his country.

3 Stephen Lawrence
In April 1993, Stephen Lawrence was waiting for a bus in Eltham in London when he and his friend were set upon by a group of white, racist young men. Stephen was stabbed twice in his upper body and he died. His murder seemed senseless, but unfortunately fitted a pattern: that year there had been another nine racially motivated killings. His parents, Doreen and Neville Lawrence, have campaigned to find their son's killers and have also set up a charity to help black students to get the education that their son longed to achieve.

It is easy to believe that racism happens in another country or in the past, but this is not the case. Racism is still a major problem in the UK today.

● STANDING UP TO RACISM

In this country, many Christians have tried to stand up against racism. When the British National Party won an election on the Isle of Dogs in London, an Anglican priest there spoke out against their racist ideas and found that his church was attacked.

Some Christians have joined groups to help support the struggle for the end of racism. One of these groups is the Evangelical Council for Racial Justice. They have set up groups in cities in the UK to help Christians think about what the Bible says about racism and to encourage them to pray and work for a better world.

The Council of Churches in Britain and Ireland set up a Community and Race Relations Unit, whose job it is to help churches of all types to campaign against racism. As well as campaigning against the racism in society, they seek to represent people from different religious and racial backgrounds who might be having problems in finding jobs or a place to live.

Jesus' call to love your neighbour as yourself continues to inspire their work.

BLACK OR WHITE?

🎧 **Winner of the Equal Rights poster competition, 1983. What is this poster trying to say?**

❓ THINK ABOUT IT!

2. How would you react to the bullying of one of your friends if it was for racial reasons? Give reasons for your answer.

3. In what other ways do you think the Church could put Jesus' words about 'loving your neighbour' into action? Give reasons for your answer.

4. 'If you have a racist friend, now is the time for this friendship to end' ('Racist Friend' by The Specials). Do you agree? Give reasons for your answer showing you have thought about it from more than one point of view.

5. Take time to reflect on the 'Black or White?' image above. How does it make you feel? Discuss your feelings with your partner and then share them with the class.

In this lesson you will:
- explore why religion and religious ideas can cause prejudice
- analyse how religious ideas might help overcome prejudice and discrimination.

DIFFERENCES BETWEEN RELIGIONS

In your RE lessons so far, you will have found out that although there are similarities between religions, there are also many differences. These differences include:
- beliefs about life after death
- views on the role of women
- beliefs about God
- ways of celebrating festivals and holy days
- ways of marking rites of passage.

Religions deal with these differences in a number of ways.
- Some believers might argue that only their religion is true and that every other religion is not.
- Others say their religion is true, but that other religions can contain truth. There is a Sikh saying: 'When man takes one step towards God, God takes a thousand steps towards man.' This saying shows how Sikhs believe God cares for his people, and there is also a similar saying in the Muslim faith.
- Other believers might say that there is some underlying truth to each religion, but they all have only a partial understanding of God or an ultimate reality.

THINK ABOUT IT!

1. Which of the three explanations opposite appeals to you most? Which appeals least? Give reasons for your answer.

RELIGIOUS DISCRIMINATION

Differences between religions can lead to prejudice and discrimination.

Anti-Semitism

Anti-Semitism is prejudice against Jewish people. In the twelfth century, Jews were banned from England. This ban lasted for three centuries. When the ban was lifted, Jews were not permitted to stand for parliament and were denied access to university because it was felt that they would corrupt the country. People treated them with disrespect and they were often blamed for the death of Jesus (even though it was the Romans who had executed him).

When Adolf Hitler came to power in Germany in 1933, he used the anti-Semitism that had existed in Europe for hundreds of years to win support for himself and his policy of mass extermination (see page 23).

Islamaphobia

Islamaphobia is an irrational fear of or discrimination against Muslims. Following the September 11th attacks, Muslims have become scapegoats because the hijackers were extremist Muslims. Muslims in the UK, and elsewhere, are often treated with suspicion and are sometimes blamed as a group for the actions carried out by the terrorists.

⊃ **In September 2001 Catholic children in North Belfast came under attack from Protestants – a modern example of religious discrimination in the UK.**

RELIGIOUS TOLERANCE?

In France, the government has recently passed a law that bans the wearing of noticeable religious symbols such as the hijab (the headdress many Muslim women wear) in schools. This could be seen as religious discrimination. However, the French government and many others argue that there should be no obvious marks of religion in schools in order to avoid offending people or highlighting religious differences.

THINK ABOUT IT!

2. Do you think the French government is right to ban the wearing of religious symbols in schools? Discuss in groups.

HOW CAN RELIGIONS WORK TOGETHER?

Many religious leaders have encouraged their followers to talk to members of other faiths in order to overcome discrimination and misunderstanding. Increasingly, people have tried to get together and understand each other's religions.

The World Council of Churches has set up a group to help Christians communicate and understand other religions. The Centre for Interfaith Dialogue was set up at Middlesex University in order to help people from different religions understand and appreciate each other.

Where does RE fit in?

Many people think that religious education in schools is a very important way to try to counter prejudices against different religions. RE introduces people to different ideas without seeking to convert them or change their minds. It also shows that the 'big questions' that religions ask are common to all cultures and countries.

THINK ABOUT IT!

3. How might religions encourage dialogue and understanding between each other? Use ideas from this lesson and your own research to help you answer this question. Ask your friends and family what they think. You could also visit the websites of the Centre for Interfaith Dialogue and the World Council of Churches. To access the sites visit www.heinemann.co.uk/hotlinks, type in the express code 7266P and click on this section.

4. Write a paragraph explaining how studying RE contributes to your understanding of different faiths and cultures? Could RE play a part in preventing prejudice and discrimination?

Pope John Paul II (left) greets Sikh religious leader Manjit Singh Sahib (centre) and Hindu religious leader Shankaracharya Madhavananda Saraswati (right) at the end of an inter-religious meeting which brought together leaders from nine different faiths, 7 November 1999.

What the task is all about:

These are quite detailed assessment activities so you may want to choose one. Your teacher will guide you.

1. Imagine that a group of people who wanted to raise awareness about the problem of racism decided to hold a special day in memory of Stephen Lawrence. Draw up a detailed plan for how they might celebrate Stephen Lawrence Day in the form of a PowerPoint presentation. What sort of events might they organise? Would there be hopeful as well as sad moments? Would there be music? Would there be a special symbol for the day? What would be the purpose of the day? How might they refer to the work of people like Martin Luther King, Gandhi and Malcolm X? Explain why you have chosen to organise the celebration in this way.

2. Use the material in chapter 2 to prepare an assembly entitled 'Did the Dream Die?' Explain why you have planned your assembly in this way.

What you need to do to complete the task:

● For question 1, you will need to do some further research about Stephen Lawrence so that you can develop some ideas about how and why he might be remembered. To access the Stephen Lawrence Charitable Trust website visit www.heinemann.co.uk/hotlinks, type in the express code 7266P and click on this section. Use the information in chapter 2 to help you make connections between the teachings of Gandhi, Martin Luther King and Malcolm X and the short life of Stephen Lawrence.

● In your presentation show that you have thought deeply about why people might want to remember what happened to Stephen Lawrence.

● For question 2, you should use information from each of the spreads not just the one about Martin Luther King. Make links between the lives and teachings of Gandhi, Martin Luther King and Malcolm X and what you have learnt about prejudice and racism, for example the Holocaust, the murder of Stephen Lawrence, the challenges to racism in schools through subjects like RE and Citizenship.

● Try to balance the content of your assembly so that people have a sense of hope as well as a feeling of sadness at some of the things that have happened.

Hints and tips

● Use your imagination for question 1. You can be as creative as you like, but remember to use the information about prejudice and racism in chapter 2.

● Use you imagination when you plan the assembly in question 2. Decide how you want to tell the story. Choose quotes that will help the audience understand the key ideas and events. You might want to use music or show film extracts, you might use drama or role play. How might you involve the audience? Do you want them to go away feeling depressed or hopeful?

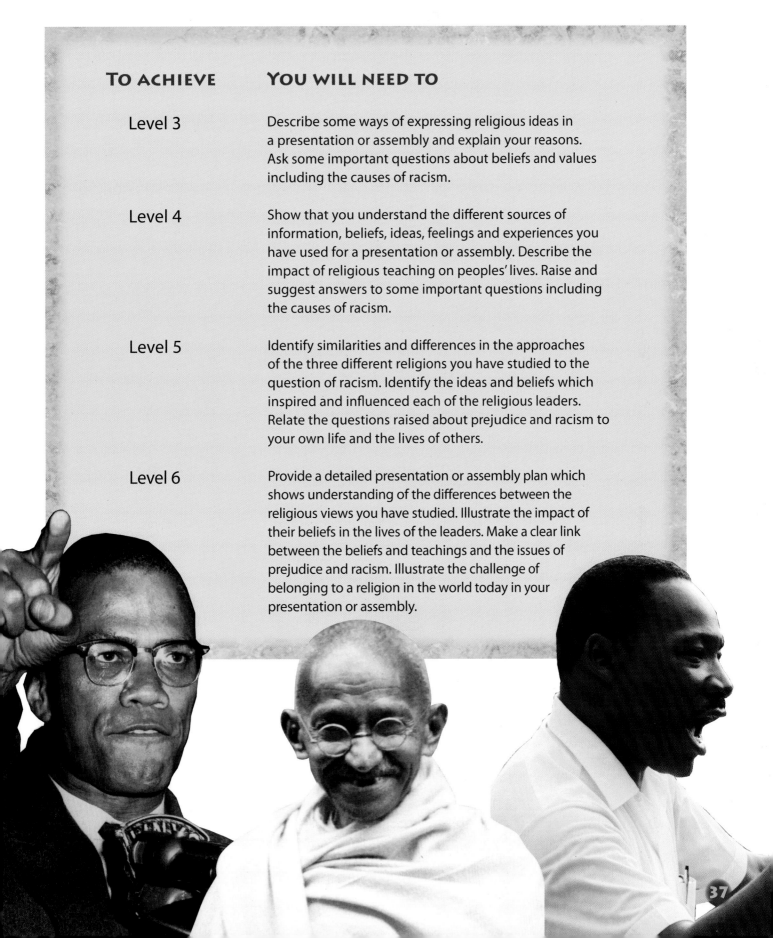

TO ACHIEVE	YOU WILL NEED TO
Level 3	Describe some ways of expressing religious ideas in a presentation or assembly and explain your reasons. Ask some important questions about beliefs and values including the causes of racism.
Level 4	Show that you understand the different sources of information, beliefs, ideas, feelings and experiences you have used for a presentation or assembly. Describe the impact of religious teaching on peoples' lives. Raise and suggest answers to some important questions including the causes of racism.
Level 5	Identify similarities and differences in the approaches of the three different religions you have studied to the question of racism. Identify the ideas and beliefs which inspired and influenced each of the religious leaders. Relate the questions raised about prejudice and racism to your own life and the lives of others.
Level 6	Provide a detailed presentation or assembly plan which shows understanding of the differences between the religious views you have studied. Illustrate the impact of their beliefs in the lives of the leaders. Make a clear link between the beliefs and teachings and the issues of prejudice and racism. Illustrate the challenge of belonging to a religion in the world today in your presentation or assembly.

3 POVERTY

THE BIGGER PICTURE

In this chapter you will be learning about poverty, its causes and some religious responses to it. You will investigate how poverty affects people and the choices they make. You will study key ideas about wealth and poverty from a variety of religious traditions.

WHAT?

You will:
- investigate what causes poverty
- learn some of the key religious teachings on poverty
- reflect on how some religious people respond to poverty
- identify the impact of sewa in Sikhism
- make connections between faith and action
- evaluate the work of two individuals from religious backgrounds who have helped the poor.

HOW?

By:
- analyzing key religious teachings about wealth and poverty
- evaluating key religious ideas such as sewa in Sikhism and liberation theology in Christianity
- exploring the lives of some prominent religious people.

WHY?

Because:
- it is important to understand the link between belief and behaviour with regards to poverty and wealth
- many people help those in need because of their religious beliefs.

Does the contrast between rich and poor in the UK make poverty more apparent than in developing countries?

KEY IDEAS

- Poverty has a number of causes and a number of consequences.
- Religious teachings and beliefs have often been used to help inspire religious people to help those in need.
- Liberation theology is a Christian way of thinking about God which encourages believers to act on the behalf of the poor.
- Sewa is the Sikh idea of service to others.
- There is a link between belief and behaviour in the area of poverty.

A young Iraqi girl finds an apple while digging through piles of rubbish at the Tajee dump.

KEY WORDS

LEDCs	MEDCs
Wealth	Poverty
Karma	Moksha
Justice	Sewa
Langar	Gurdwara
Khalsa	Emergency aid
Developing countries	Long-term aid
Liberation theology	

Does the number of people living in poverty in Africa make the problem more urgent than in the UK?

In this lesson you will:
- explore different reasons why poverty exists
- reflect on two religious responses to the issue of poverty
- express your own ideas about why there is poverty.

The *New Oxford English Dictionary* defines the word 'poor' as:

> 'Lacking sufficient money to live at a standard considered normal or comfortable.'

The question is why are people poor? Over the centuries, there have been a number of reasons given for why people are poor.

- lack natural resources
- natural disasters such as floods or famines
- war which destroys homes and crops
- lack of education
- mounting debts
- corrupt leadership.

Poorer countries are sometimes referred to as **LEDCs** (less economically developed countries). Countries such as the USA and the UK, meanwhile, are referred to as **MEDCs** (more economically developed countries).

MEDCS are wealthy and have enough resources and skills to trade with other countries to build their **wealth**. However, even in these rich countries, there are many people who live in **poverty**. This might be because they are in low-paid jobs, are unemployed or have been made homeless.

● WHAT IS THE SOLUTION?

- Karl Marx, the political philosopher, believed that the rich should be forced to share their wealth with people in society to make things equal and just.
- Other political thinkers have argued that if trade between nations were free, it would enable LEDCs to share in the wealth.
- Other people argue that governments have a duty to look after and care for the poor.

◖ Poverty exists in rich countries like the UK as well as in developing countries.

● THE HINDU POINT OF VIEW

Hindus believe that being poor is the result of violating the laws of nature. Individually, poverty may be due to our **karma**, the consequences of irresponsible actions in a previous life. On a collective level, greed and exploitation of nature's resources also creates poverty. The Hindu holy books teach us to be responsible and to look after the resources we have been given. Karma also teaches us by showing us the consequences of our actions. Hindus try to become free from lust and greed, and to fix the mind on the divine. In this way, they achieve **moksha**, freedom from the cycle of birth and death.

THINK ABOUT IT!

1. Hindu holy books tell us of two dangers – greed and poverty. Why are greed and poverty considered to be dangerous? How could this be related to the idea of karma?

● THE CHRISTIAN POINT OF VIEW

Some Christians believe that one of the causes of poverty is the actions of the poor themselves for God rewards those who are good and punishes those who are bad. This does not, however, explain the plight of those who lead a good life but still suffer poverty, like Job for example who lost all his camels. Mother Teresa suggested that even in the face of poverty God's face can be seen and responded to. It is a Christian duty to wrestle with this and find a way to respond.

The main reason given by the Bible for poverty, however, is that the rich have lived unjust lives, which leads to the suffering of others. In the Old Testament, there are accounts of the lives and teachings of people who are called prophets. Their job was to speak God's words to the people, to challenge them to live better lives and to encourage them with hopes of a better future. One of these prophets was Amos, who was originally a shepherd. He condemned the rich and powerful of his day saying that they 'sell the needy for a pair of sandals.' (Amos 2: 6).

🎧 **Does television make us more aware of poverty and its causes?**

THINK ABOUT IT!

2. Write a title for the photograph above and then use the photograph as the centre of a mind-map on the question 'Why is there poverty?'

3. Edmund Burke (1729–97) was a British politician and political philosopher who spoke out against indifference: 'All that is necessary for the triumph of evil is for good people to do nothing.'
   a) What do you think Edmund Burke meant?
   b) How might it apply to people's attitudes and actions to the poor?

4. Create a poster or wall display that illustrates why there is poverty in the world.

3.2 WHAT DOES JUDAISM TEACH ABOUT POVERTY?

In this lesson you will:
- reflect on Jewish beliefs about and teachings on poverty
- consider the relevance of the story of Naboth's vineyard in the modern world
- make links between Jewish teaching and the world today.

NABOTH'S VINEYARD (1 KINGS 21)

Naboth's vineyard is a story from the Old Testament that reveals a great deal about Jewish ideas of ensuring **justice** for all people.

❶ King Ahab's palace was next to a vineyard owned by a man called Naboth. One day the king suggested that Naboth should sell his vineyard to him and for a generous sum. However, there was a law in Israel that forbade the selling of inherited property to the king. Naboth told the king that he could not sell him the vineyard because he had inherited it.

❷ Ahab returned to the palace upset. His wife, Queen Jezebel, decided that she would get Naboth's vineyard for her husband.

❸ She hired two men to lie at a public meeting, accusing Naboth of having spoken against both God and the king. It was a sin to speak against God and the king, and doing so would result in a death sentence. The two men did what the Queen ordered and the elders of the area put Naboth to death.

❹ God was angry and ordered the prophet Elijah to tell the king that he needed to change his ways.

❺ Elijah challenged King Ahab, and he accepted that his greed had resulted in Naboth's murder.

● JEWISH TEACHING ON THE POOR

Judaism has much to say about how poor people should be treated. Moses was given a number of instructions by God to make sure that the poor and the vulnerable were looked after. As the people of Israel had been slaves when they were in Egypt, it was important that they remembered this in their dealings with others who might have been similarly ill-treated.

The prophets – spokespeople of God's message – called on the rich and powerful to change the way they dealt with the poor. One of these prophets was Amos, who wrote:

> 'If there is a poor man among your brothers...do not be hard-hearted or tight-fisted towards your poor brother. Rather be open-handed and freely lend him whatever he needs.'
>
> *Deuteronomy 15: 7–8*

> 'You trample on the poor and force him to give you grain. Therefore, though you have built stone mansions, you will not live in them; though you have planted lush vineyards, you will not drink their wine. For I know how many are your offences and how great your sins. You oppress the righteous and take bribes and you deprive the poor of justice in the courts.'
>
> *Amos 5: 11–12*

To this day Jews believe that since all possessions are given to us by God we are never the ultimate owner and have a duty to share our wealth. Organizations like Jewish Care encourage Jewish people to give to charity in order to help those in need.

Another Jewish teaching states that every seven years, loans must be cancelled if they have not been repaid so that people are not crippled by debt. This became known as the idea of Jubliee and ties in with the belief that wealth should be shared. This Jewish teaching has inspired people campaigning about Third World debt to call for debts to be cancelled. The Jubilee Campaign continues to help put pressure on governments around the world in order to help those in need to escape from the poverty cycle, where countries are unable to pay the debts they already have and end up taking on more.

3.3 WHAT DOES CHRISTIANITY TEACH ABOUT POVERTY AND WEALTH?

In this lesson you will:
● reflect on Jesus' teaching about wealth
● express your own responses to Jesus' teaching
● apply the teachings to the way Christians live today
● evaluate the difficulties the teachings might cause for some Christians.

● WHAT DID JESUS TEACH ABOUT MONEY?

Jesus taught a great deal about money and the problems he thought that becoming obsessed with it could cause.

> 'No one can serve two masters. Either he will hate the one and love the other, or he will be devoted to the one and despise the other. You cannot serve both God and Money.'
>
> *Matthew 6: 24*

> 'It is easier for a camel to go through the eye of a needle than for a rich man to enter the kingdom of God.'
>
> *Mark 10: 25*

THINK ABOUT IT!

1. What do you think Jesus means by these quotations?

2. What is your response to these quotations?

● JESUS' ENCOUNTER WITH ZACCHAEUS (LUKE 19)

Jesus was travelling through Jericho, where a man called Zacchaeus lived. Zacchaeus was a tax collector, very rich but not very tall. Tax collectors were hated because they often took much more money than they should have done. They also worked for the Romans, whom many Israelites hated because they had taken control of Israel. Zacchaeus wanted to see Jesus, but he had to climb a tree because he would not be able to see over the crowd.

Jesus saw him in the tree and said to him, 'Zacchaeus, come down from the tree. I want to have a meal with you.'

Zacchaeus hurried down and welcomed Jesus into his home. Everyone grumbled, 'This man Zacchaeus is a sinner! And Jesus is going to eat with him.'

Later that day, Zacchaeus stood up and said to Jesus, 'I will give half of my property to the poor. I will now repay people back four times as much as I ever cheated from them.'

Jesus said to Zacchaeus, 'Today, you and your family have been saved.'

THINK ABOUT IT!

3. How had Zacchaeus acted unfairly until he met Jesus? How did he change?

4. Draw a feelings graph like the one below to show how Zacchaeus felt about his encounter with Jesus.

5. What do you think this story teaches Christians today about the use of money?

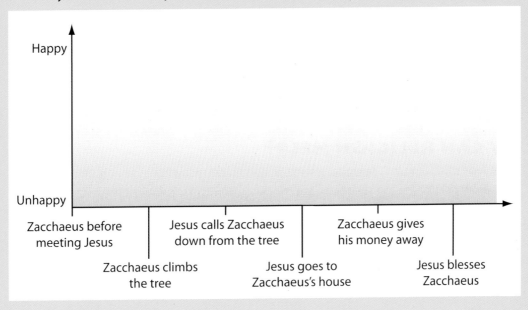

HOW DO CHRISTIANS VIEW JESUS' TEACHINGS ON MONEY TODAY?

Christians have often found it difficult to live out the teachings of Jesus about money and possessions. Some have argued that much of Jesus' teaching on wealth was to particular people who were especially concerned about money. Paul, writing in one of his letters to his friend Timothy, said

> 'For the love of money is a root of all kinds of evil. Some people, eager for money, have wandered from the faith and pierced themselves with many griefs.'
>
> *1 Timothy 6: 10*

Some Christians, meanwhile, have suggested that a mark of God's blessing is to have lots of money, although in return for that blessing all Christians have a duty to give according to their means. Most Christians find that the words of Jesus are a challenge to them to think about whether they are living their lives in a selfish way or if they are truly living in a way that helps the poor. that it is not money itself that is evil, but obsession with money. It is the love of money that Christians want to challenge. As Jesus once told his followers, people cannot serve two masters, God and money. They have to make a choice.

THINK ABOUT IT!

6. 'For the love of money is a root of all kinds of evil.' Do you agree? Give reasons for your answer, showing that you have thought about more than one point of view.

7. 'I don't care too much for money. Money can't buy me love.' (The Beatles) Were the Beatles right? Can money buy happiness?

WHAT DOES SIKHISM TEACH ABOUT POVERTY?

In this lesson you will:
- investigate the life of Bhai Puran Singh Ji
- reflect on how Bhai Puran Singh Ji was influenced by his beliefs
- identify how Sikh beliefs might have an impact on the world today.

KEY WORDS

Sewa Sikh requirement to help others

Langar Kitchen and dining hall in a gurdwara and the food served

Gurdwara A Sikh place of worship

Khalsa The Sikh community, literally meaning 'the community of the pure'

POVERTY IN INDIA

India is one of the poorer countries in the world. Problems associated with poverty in India include:
- disease
- lack of clean water
- lack of food – malnutrition.

HOW CAN RELIGION HELP?

One of the key ideas in Sikhism is **sewa** or service. Sewa can be shown in:
- tan (physical service)
- man (mental service, such as studying to help others)
- dhan (material service, where you give money to help others).

Sikhs should show sewa without expecting a reward. One way of showing sewa, for example, is to serve in the **langar** at the **gurdwara**. The langar is a kitchen where a meal is provided to all people, whether Sikh or non-Sikh.

WHO WAS BHAI PURAN SINGH JI?

One Sikh who tried to do something to help his people has been described as 'the single Sikh hero of this century (twentieth century)'.

This hero was Bhai Puran Singh Ji (later renamed Bhagat Puran Singh Ji). He was born in 1904 in India and was raised as a Hindu. In his early life he travelled around, stopping in Hindu temples whenever he could. One day, whilst at a Hindu temple, he was asked to clean out the temple by some of the priests.

When he had finished the work, the priests sat in front of him and started to eat without offering him any food, even though he was hungry and had just cleaned the temple.

The next place he stayed was a gurdwara – a Sikh temple. The leader of the gurdwara gave him food and milk to drink. Then he found Bhai Puran Singh Ji a place to sleep without asking for anything in return. This persuaded Bhai Puran Singh Ji to become a Sikh, and it was not long before he joined the **Khalsa** – the brotherhood of Sikhs.

Bhagat Puran Singh Ji (1904–92).

THINK ABOUT IT!

1. Do you think Bhai Puran Singh Ji should have been given food by the Hindu priests he had been working for? Give reasons for your answer.

WHAT DID BHAI PURAN SINGH JI DO NEXT?

Bhai Puran Singh Ji decided to give his life to helping people in need. He not only helped the living, but on the many occasions when he came across bodies of humans or animals who lay where they had died, he prepared a grave and buried them, believing the dead deserved respect as well as the living.

Bhai Puran Singh Ji was given the title Bhagat Puran Singh Ji ('Bhagat' means 'saint') to recognize his great work and leadership.

THINK ABOUT IT!

2. 'Dignity in death is a birthright of each living thing.'
   a) What do you think Bhagat Puran Singh meant by this?
   b) How might this be put into practice in this country and in poorer countries?

THE INSTITUTE

In 1947, Bhagat Puran Singh Ji decided to open an institute to care for the suffering people he came across. He gave all his money to this project and encouraged others to do the same. This institute is still open in Amritsar in India, and is now run by people who he inspired to help the poor as he had done.

As well as caring for the poor and sick, Bhagat Puran Singh Ji was also a campaigner for environmental causes. He realized that things such as pollution and soil erosion were in part to blame for poverty. He did what he could to inform people about these issues. One of the campaigns he led tried to persuade all people in the Punjab region of northern India to plant at least one tree in order to help the planet and the people on it. This helps because trees produce oxygen which supports life.

Bhagat Puran Singh Ji died in 1992, but his followers still carry on his work.

Bhagat Puran Singh Ji with one of the people he helped at Pingalwara, the institute he opened in Amritsar in India.

THINK ABOUT IT!

3. Explain how Bhagat Puran Singh Ji's Sikh beliefs inspired him to do what he did.

4. Imagine you are a radio journalist. You have been asked to write a script to introduce a show about the life of Bhagat Puran Singh Ji. Use the information on these pages to write your script. Remember to include information about his beliefs and work. You could use your answer to question 3 to help you with this.

In this lesson you will:
- investigate projects designed to help people in the long term
- evaluate the need for and success of these projects
- form your own arguments about the need to help those suffering as a result of poverty and persuade others of your opinion.

KEY WORDS

Emergency aid Help given to people or countries in a crisis

Long-term aid Money or other help given to a person, community or country to help overcome a long-term problem

Developing countries Countries who are developing their economies and often experience great hardship

● LONG-TERM AID

When an area or a country faces a particular disaster, such as a flood or a famine, it needs **emergency aid** to help people immediately. This type of aid might consist of food and medical supplies. However, there also needs to be a commitment to **long-term aid**. This means continuing to support a country so that it can rebuild itself. Examples of long-term aid might include:

- providing agricultural equipment
- establishing schools
- providing water pumps and wells.

The ultimate aim of long-term aid is to enable the country to manage on its own. It can also help individuals to help themselves, giving them dignity and respect.

🎧 **The photo on the left shows a child sleeping on the streets in Mumbai. The photo on the right shows Haitian women in the aftermath of a flood which killed over 20,000 people. Which of these people requires long-term aid?**

● TRAIDCRAFT

One of the biggest problems for people in **developing countries** is getting a fair price for what they produce. Many sell to large companies who pay rock bottom prices. They accept these prices because they know that if they refuse to sell to them, there are plenty who will take their place. If crops like coffee, cocoa or sugar cane remain unsold, they are worthless. There really is little choice but to sell for a low price.

Traidcraft products can be bought in many British supermarkets nowadays. Even though they might be a little more expensive, at least people who buy their products know that the producers are earning a fair price for their goods rather than being exploited by big businesses.

Traidcraft

Fair trade differs from standard trade in five principal ways. As a Christian organization committed to fair trade, Traidcraft:

- focuses on trading with producer groups who are poor, helping them develop skills and sustainable livelihoods through the trading relationship
- pays fair prices that cover the full cost of production and enables a living wage and other fair rewards to be earned by producers
- provides credit when needed to allow orders to be fulfilled, and pays premiums to be used to provide further benefits to producer communities
- encourages the fair treatment of all workers, ensuring good conditions in the workplace and throughout the supply chain
- aims to build up long-term relationships rather than looking for short-term commercial advantage.

● THE BIG ISSUE

You might have seen people selling a magazine called *The Big Issue* on the streets of Britain. You might even have bought a copy.

The Big Issue was started as a charity by two businessmen as a way of helping homeless people to help themselves. Sellers of *The Big Issue* are homeless or at serious risk of becoming homeless. They are given ten copies every week and use the money they earn from selling those ten to buy more. The more they sell, the more they can buy and the more profit they make. How they spend their profits from selling the magazines is entirely up to them. Whilst selling *The Big Issue* might not provide enough money to pay for all they need, at least they are given a chance to earn money and feel like useful members of the community.

🎧 **Is providing long-term aid to people in need in the UK as important as providing long-term aid to developing countries?**

? THINK ABOUT IT!

1. **a)** 'Long-term aid is important to people suffering hardship.' Do you agree or disagree? Give reasons for your answer.
   b) In your own words explain how either Traidcraft or *The Big Issue* provides long-term aid for people suffering hardship.

2. Using the information about Traidcraft and *The Big Issue*, do one of the following.
   a) Write a letter to your local shopkeeper, persuading him or her to stock fair trade products.
   b) Write a letter to a friend persuading them to buy *The Big Issue* regularly.
   c) Produce an ad campaign for either fair trade products or *The Big Issue*.

3. 'All countries should abolish their space exploration programmes and use the money to wipe out poverty instead.' Discuss this statement in small groups, showing that you have thought about more than one point of view.

In this lesson you will:
- explain the importance of the Parable of the Sheep and the Goats for Christians to help them reflect on their need to help the poor and the powerless
- make links between Christian belief and relief work
- explore how Tearfund works in the developing world to help people.

THE PARABLE OF THE SHEEP AND THE GOATS

Parables are stories that are told to help people understand and remember important teachings. Jesus told a number of parables. One of these was the Parable of the Sheep and the Goats. The Parable is about how, at the final judgement, God will separate good people from bad people as a shepherd divides sheep from goats.

'All the nations of the world will be gathered together at the end of time before God. The Son of man [Jesus] will divide the people into two groups, just as a shepherd separates their sheep from their goats.

He will put the righteous people on his right side and say to them, "Come, take the Kingdom with me. I was hungry and you fed me. I was thirsty and you gave me a drink. I was a stranger and you received me into your home, naked and you clothed me, sick and you took care of me; in jail and you visited me."

The righteous asked when they had done these things. The Son of Man replied, "I tell you, whenever you did this for the least of people, you did it for me."

Then the Son of Man said to the people on his left: "Away from me – you did not feed me, give me a drink or clothe me; you did not welcome me when I was a stranger or care for me when I was sick or in jail."

The people on the left said to the Son of Man, "When did we do this to you?"

"When you did not do it for the least of people, you did not help me. Be off with you – to an eternal punishment."'

Matthew 25: 31–46 (adapted)

THINK ABOUT IT!

1. How does the parable of the sheep and the goats encourage Christians to help the poor?

2. Is the fear of or belief in a judgement after death a good reason to do good things in this life? Give reasons for your answer.

3. How do you think these beliefs might inspire Christians to act?

4. Describe an instance when you helped someone and explain your reasons for doing so.

TEARFUND

The Parable of the Sheep and the Goats has encouraged many Christians to act to help the poor and the disadvantaged in practical ways as they respond to the idea that in helping others they might be helping Jesus.

In the late 1960s, the Christian organization The Evangelical Alliance set up a relief fund to help people in the developing world. This eventually became known as Tearfund.

Tearfund works with partner organizations in the developing world to help the poor and other vulnerable members of society. They have given emergency aid to help people in areas affected by natural disasters such as floods or famine, as well as people who are victims of wars and prejudice.

> Ten-year-old Hannah wants to be a doctor. 'I want to help people,' she says.
>
> School helps children grow in confidence, gain life skills and find work when they are older. And that benefits the whole community. But without education, people become trapped in a cycle of poverty, starvation and bad health.
>
> And yet, for the first time, education has come to the remote valley in Ethiopia where Hannah lives. At last she has the opportunity to fulfil her dream.
>
> Tearfund website

Tearfund relief worker monitoring child malnutrition as part of a mother and child supplementary food programme in Rumbek, southern Sudan.

THINK ABOUT IT!

5. Draw a diagram to highlight the work of Tearfund. This could be in the form of a spider diagram. If it helps, add symbols or images to your diagram to remind you of key aspects. You could use a copy of their magazine *Tear Times* or their website to help you. To access the Tearfund website visit www.heinemann.co.uk/hotlinks, type in the express code 7266P and click on this section.

Tearfund also provide long-term aid, for example:

● literacy classes
● clean water and sanitation
● drug rehabilitation.

Supporters of Tear Fund feel that there is a connection between some of the problems the developing world face and the beliefs they hold. One example they give is of an African tribe that believed an area was contaminated with evil spirits. Workers from Tearfund shared their Christian faith and the people of the village accepted it as their own. They decided that they should dig a well in the area they had believed to be evil: it proved to be the best source for water in the area!

Tearfund has also helps people in the UK by training unemployed people and running child care projects in poor areas.

In this lesson you will:
● understand the term 'liberation theology'
● explore events in the life of Oscar Romero
● evaluate the work of Oscar Romero and the reasons for his actions.

LIBERATION THEOLOGY

Liberation theology is the belief that God is biased in favour of the poor and that Christians should seek to help the poor to be free. For some Christians, this means that they should get involved in politics – either by campaigning for a party or, if necessary, by getting involved in an armed struggle for justice.

Liberation theology began in some of the poorer countries of South America, originally in Roman Catholic churches. Today, it is a way of looking at the Christian life that now influences many different churches in many different countries.

A BRAVE MAN

Oscar Romero was an Archbishop in El Salvador who spoke out for human rights during the civil war there. As more and more people died, Romero became popular with the poor people he tried to defend. His church services were well attended and broadcast on the radio throughout the country. Bravely, he spoke out against those who were killing their own people. He even criticized other church leaders who did not share his horror at what was happening. His actions, however, put his life in danger.

> ‘If they succeed in killing me, I forgive and bless those who do it. Hopefully they will realize they are wasting their time. A bishop will die, but the Church of God, which is the people, will never perish.’

These words were spoken by Oscar Romero, the Archbishop of San Salvador in El Salvador. A few days later, on 24 March 1980, he was shot dead whilst leading worship in a small hospital chapel in El Salvador.

Archbishop Oscar Romero of El Salvador, an outspoken proponent of human rights.

1917 Oscar Romero was born in El Salvador, a small country in Central America. Whilst some rich people live in El Salvador, most of the people are very poor.

1929 When he was twelve years old, Oscar Romero worked for a carpenter. However, his faith in Roman Catholic Christianity was so important to him that he decided to train to be a priest.

1961 A civil war broke out in El Salvador that would last until 1991. A civil war is when two groups of people are fighting for control of their country.

1977 Oscar Romero became the Archbishop of San Salvador. This made him one of the most important religious leaders in his country.

THINK ABOUT IT!

1. Do you think Oscar Romero was right in what he did? Give reasons for your answer.

2. 'Whatever you did not do for one of the least of these, you did not do for me.' (Matthew 25: 45)
   a) What do you think this quotation means?
   b) How would Oscar Romero respond to this quotation? Give evidence for your point of view.

El Salvador

1977 A priest called Rutilio Grande was murdered along with an old man and a seven-year-old child. A few weeks later, another priest, Father Alfonso Navarro, was shot dead. Oscar Romero demanded an enquiry into these four killings. The government refused.

'The disciples said, "See, Lord, here are two swords."

"That is enough," he replied.'

Luke 22: 38

1978 Thousands of people were killed, a million people were made homeless and nearly twenty per cent of the population fled the country because of the war.

THINK ABOUT IT!

3. Look at the quote above. To what extent can a Christian use force to overcome tyranny?

1980 Oscar Romero was killed whilst leading a church service. He was shot at the moment in the communion service when he was holding up the bread, a symbol of the sacrifice of Christ's body.

What the task is all about:

1. Imagine you are a reviewer and write a review of Chapter 3 for a magazine aimed at raising the awareness of young people from different religious backgrounds about world poverty. Give your view of the strengths and weaknesses of the chapter and end by saying whether you would recommend it as a useful resource for people interested in learning more about different views of poverty and how to fight it.

2. The writer of the review (that's you) has received a letter from a humanist saying that they felt left out because, 'you don't have to be religious to care about poverty'. How will you reply to the letter?

3. 'Religion should keep out of politics.' What do you think? Write an answer explaining your own view and showing how people from two different religions might respond to this statement.

What you need to do to complete the task:

- Look back at Chapter 3 and make notes on each of the spreads, deciding which you want to refer to in your review and what you will say about them.

- Make sure that you can explain the Christian, Jewish, Muslim and Sikh beliefs about poverty that you have looked at in this chapter.

- You may need to research the humanist view on poverty in order to answer question 2. To access the British Humanist Association's website visit www.heinemann.co.uk/hotlinks, type in the express code 7266P and click on this section.

Hints and tips

- Remember that as a reviewer you are expected to take a critical view, express your own opinion and back it up with evidence.

- Note that the readers of the magazine belong to different religions and will want to know whether more than one view is represented.

TO ACHIEVE	YOU WILL NEED TO
Level 3	Describe the different religious teachings covered in chapter 3 and say whether it is a useful resource for teaching about poverty or not. Ask some questions regarding beliefs about poverty. Show that you can see things from someone else's point of view.
Level 4	Show that you understand the different religious views on poverty and that you can evaluate the chapter, giving reasons for your views. Express the views of someone from a different stand point.
Level 5	Explain the similarities and differences between the beliefs of different religions on poverty. Produce a detailed evaluation of chapter 3 and give your own views about its value as a resource, giving reasons for your views. Present a reasoned argument from the someone else's point of view.
Level 6	Write a detailed, critical evaluation using examples to show the strengths and weaknesses of the chapter. Express your own views and opinions about the issue of world poverty and show that you have insights into the beliefs and opinions of others and the differences between them.

4 WAR AND PEACE

THE BIGGER PICTURE

In this chapter you will investigate ideas about war and peace. You will explore differing religious views on war and peace in Christianity, Judaism and Buddhism. Finally, you will reflect on whether pacifism (the belief in non-violence) is a possibility in today's world.

WHAT?

You will:

- investigate possible reasons for war and responses to them, including religious responses
- reflect upon the possible effects war has on people
- evaluate whether people should fight or not
- explore the beliefs and teachings of Christianity, Judaism and Buddhism about war and peace.

HOW?

By:

- discussing reasons for war and responses to them
- comparing religious teachings about war and peace, especially in Christianity, Judaism and Buddhism
- expressing your own views on whether or not it is ever right to go to war
- considering the example of people who refuse to fight in a war.

WHY?

Because:

- war is a reality of life in the early twenty-first century
- religious people often have strong views about war and peace
- it will help you to make decisions about war and to understand the world in which you live.

KEY IDEAS

- War has existed for almost as long as humankind has existed.
- Civilians as well as soldiers suffer and die in wars.
- Wars allow people to show great bravery, both by fighting and by not fighting.
- Religions have strong views on war and peace that can be interpreted differently.
- Some religious people have been persecuted in wars, for example the Jews in the Second World War.
- Some religious people have used war to their advantage, for example, the Crusades or the Hebrew conquest of the Promised Land.
- The ideas of the just war and the holy war are rooted in religious teaching.
- All religions teach about the importance of peace whilst some justify war as well.

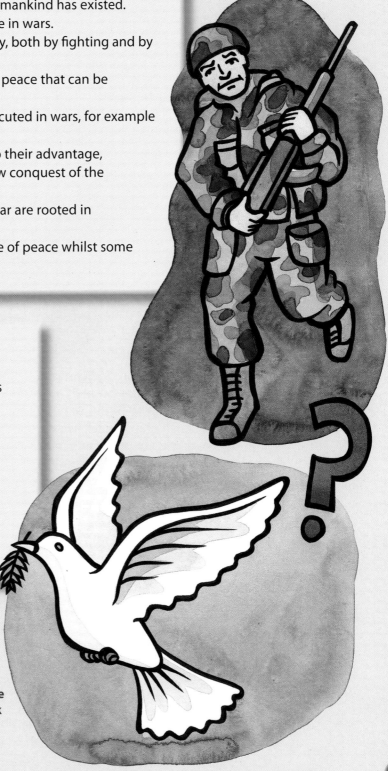

KEY WORDS

War	Conscientious objectors
Pacifists	Just war
Tyranny	Holy war
Crusades	Ahimsa
Persecute	Prophets
Terrorism	Dalai Lama
Exile	Monasteries

Religious attitudes to war are often inconsistent. Do you think it is ever right to go to war?

In this lesson you will:
● empathize with soldiers in the D-Day landings
● begin to explore whether the Christian Church should support soldiers at war.

● THE D-DAY LANDINGS, 1944

In June 2004, a small army of veteran soldiers visited Northern France. They wanted to mark the fact that on 6 June 1944 thousands of young men landed small craft, under heavy enemy fire, on the beaches there. Their mission was to drive the invading **Nazi** army back and to free the people of France from Nazi rule. On that one day alone, more than 4500 allied soldiers (mainly British and American) died.

Had these men not given their lives to free France, the Nazi army might have invaded Britain from France. A further 400,000 soldiers from both sides were killed or injured in the following weeks and months as the allies drove the Germans back inland.

Ed Gorman (see photo) is an American who was involved in the D-Day landings. As his landing craft neared the beach, it was hit by a German mine. This jammed the door of the craft, which meant that it could not land. The crew, including Ed, desperately tried to repair the door so they could land.

Whilst doing this, they watched the carnage unfold on the beach. They witnessed hundreds of young men being killed or injured within minutes of landing, knowing that if the mine had not damaged their craft, they would have been amongst them. Eventually they managed to land, but Ed Gorman still does not feel he can tell the whole story of what happened.

Daily Telegraph, 5 June 2004

THINK ABOUT IT!

1. Draw a 'senses spider diagram' based on the account of D-Day above.
   a) In five minutes, write at least three key words for each leg: what you saw, heard, touched, smelt, tasted and your feelings.
   b) Use *all* the key words you have written on your senses mind map to write a paragraph describing what you think D-Day was like.

2. Why do you think Ed Gorman still cannot talk about what happened once he had landed on the beach in France?

WHY DOES WAR HAPPEN?

Historians have studied the events leading up to the Second World **War** and come up with many theories as to why it happened. There is little overall agreement! What most people do not argue with though is that once Hitler's armies had shown their intentions to invade and rule most of Europe, they had to be stopped. Fighting fire with fire was the only real option. This is why armies of young men, with the support of most of the rest of the population, fought and lost their lives.

CONSCIENTIOUS OBJECTORS

Some people disagreed with the war and refused to fight. These people were called **conscientious objectors**. Often they would not fight because they believed it was wrong to kill other human beings. They have also been termed **pacifists** because they preferred peaceful rather than violent methods of resolving issues.

Some conscientious objectors refused to fight but would take part in the war effort. Some signed up as doctors, nurses and stretcher-bearers. Others stayed at home and worked in factories, making weapons or producing food. Everybody pulled together.

WHAT DID THE CHURCH DO?

In Britain, many members of the Christian Church supported the war effort and were encouraged to do so by Christian leaders. Regiments of soldiers had their own priests or chaplains, and the churches back home were full of families praying that their loved ones would return and that the war would soon be won.

Many Christians believed that by fighting, or helping the war effort by working in factories, they were doing what God wanted them to, even though the weapons were designed to kill.

THINK ABOUT IT!

3. Do you think the Christian Church should support soldiers at war? Give at least two reasons for your opinion.

🔊 **The D-Day landings helped secure victory for the allies in World War II at the cost of thousands of young men's lives. Do you think it was worth the loss?**

In this lesson you will:
● analyze and apply the ideas of the just war and the holy war
● evaluate the ideas of the just war and the holy war.

KEY WORDS

Just war Theory about when it is morally acceptable to fight a war

Tyranny Extreme government or ruler imposing their will on people

Holy war A war justified by religious reasons and fought on behalf of God or the religious community

Crusades War between Christians and Muslims (11th–13th centuries)

Ahimsa Non-violence, respect for life

IS THERE SUCH A THING AS A JUST WAR?

For almost as long as the human race has been on the Earth, people have argued over whether or not it is ever right to fight a war. Some wars might need to be fought, but how could they be seen as being morally right?

Since the time of the Christian thinker Thomas Aquinas (1225–74), Christians have talked about a **just war**, a war that it is better to fight than not. To be a just war, the war must match the five criteria on the spider diagram below.

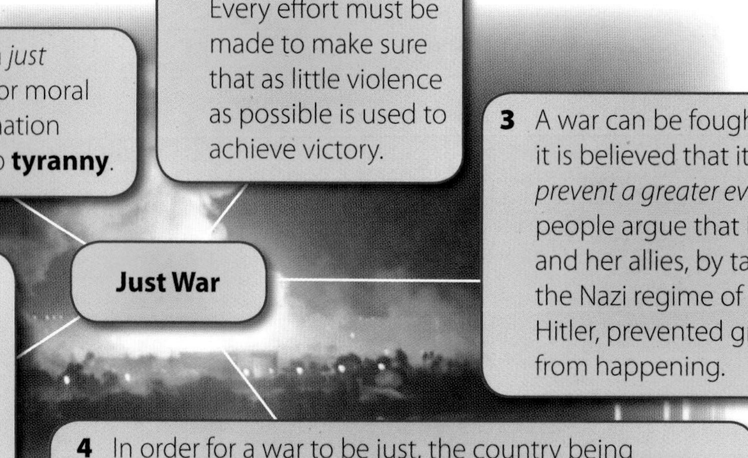

JUST WAR

1 The war must be fought for a *just cause*. There has to be a just or moral reason such as defending a nation under attack or trying to stop **tyranny**.

2 There must be *controlled violence*. Every effort must be made to make sure that as little violence as possible is used to achieve victory.

3 A war can be fought if it is believed that it would *prevent a greater evil*. Most people argue that Britain and her allies, by taking on the Nazi regime of Adolf Hitler, prevented great evil from happening.

Just War

5 The force used in the war should be *proportional*. Proportional means that the amount of force used should not be more than necessary. The military should also try to avoid injuring or killing innocent **civilians**.

4 In order for a war to be just, the country being defended must be under the *control of the leader of the country* and not just dominated by the military in the war zone. They can make only minor decisions; the politicians must make the most important decisions.

? THINK ABOUT IT!

1. Draw a spider diagram like the one above with 'Just war' in the middle and the italicized words/phrases on each leg. Turn it into a mind map by drawing a small symbol to represent each of the words/phrases.

2. Do you think that a just war is possible in the world we live in today? Explain your answer.

HOLY WAR

Many different religions have taught that there are times when it is right to fight. In the Old Testament, the Jews often practised a **holy war** policy. They believed that God was calling them to wage war against those who did not belong to their religion.

During the **Crusades** (eleventh to thirteenth centuries), both Christians and Muslims believed they were fighting a holy war for their God.

For many people, a holy war should have three elements:

1 It must have a religious goal.

2 A religious leader must authorize the war.

3 There must be a religious or spiritual reward. This is usually a promise that God will look after people who fight and die in a war for their religion.

↻ **A painting by Philip James depicting the battle between Richard I Lionheart (1157–99) and Saladin (1137–93) in Palestine during the Crusades.**

WHICH IS BETTER: JUST WAR OR HOLY WAR?

- Many people favour the just war over the holy war.
- Some favour no war at all.
- Most Buddhists and Hindus are against war because fighting goes against their belief in **ahimsa** (non-violence). However, if they feel the cause is just, for example if the war is being fought to defend themselves, their nation or their faith, many will fight.

THINK ABOUT IT!

3. Can a war ever be holy? Give two reasons for 'yes' and two reasons for 'no'.

4. Do you think religion causes war? Give reasons for your answer.

4.3 SIMON WIESENTHAL – GOD'S AVENGER OF EVIL?

In this lesson you will:
- investigate events in the life of Simon Wiesenthal
- evaluate the life and work of Simon Wiesenthal.

KEY WORDS

Persecute To bully people often due to prejudice

● WHO WAS SIMON WIESENTHAL?

Every war creates heroes and heroines whose stories illustrate just how terrible war can be. Although many of these people are involved in the fighting, there are others who are involved in other ways. Simon Wiesenthal is one of these people. His story illustrates just what can happen in times of war when human rights seem to be forgotten.

Read about the things that happened in his life which inspired his actions after 1945:

1908 I was born in the country now called the Ukraine. My parents were Jewish and I was proud to follow their religion as well.

1932 I graduated from university. I had to go to Czechoslovakia to study, and then I moved to Poland.

1936 A joyous year. I married a gorgeous Jewish girl called Cyla.

1939 Dreadful news. The Russians have started to **persecute** the Jews in Poland. Why? I don't know – I am just a Jew trying to live the way God wants me to.

1941 The Nazis have taken control from the Russians. I was sent to a prison camp and then a work camp, even though I am sure I have done nothing wrong.

1942 89 people from mine and Cyla's families have been killed by the Nazis. When will it all end? I arranged for Cyla to take a non-Jewish identity to give her a better chance of surviving. She has had to leave me – I hope this saves her life.

1943 I spent some time in a **concentration camp** but I managed to escape. I think God must be looking after me!

1944 My freedom did not last long. I was recaptured. I found out that 149,000 people had died in my camp. How can people do that to us just because we are Jews? We are still human beings like they are. The Russians have recaptured the camp from the Nazis. A guard told me they are keeping a few of us alive so they have some people to guard. They will be sent to fight otherwise!

1945 I left the concentration camp. Along with the 33 other remaining prisoners, we were marched hundreds of miles across Europe to a camp in Austria.

5 May 1945 A wonderful day! The Americans have taken control of the camp. We are free! Thank God!

Nov 1945 My beautiful wife Cyla has survived. We are back together!

🎧 **Prisoners in Dachau, a Nazi concentration camp, in 1945.**

62

1. Simon and Cyla were both proud of the fact they were Jews. Do you think Cyla was right to take on a new non-Jewish identity to save her life? Explain your answer.

2. Was Simon Wiesenthal a hero? Give reasons for your answer.

The rest of Simon Wiesenthal's life has been dedicated to tracking down the Nazis who were responsible for the murders of some of the six million Jews who died during the Second World War (1939–45). In 1959, he managed to track down Adolf Eichmann, the mastermind behind the policy of killing the Jews. After a trial, in 1961, Eichmann was executed for mass murder.

To this day, the Wiesenthal Centre in Los Angeles, staffed by Simon himself and some of those who have been inspired by his life and work, is continuing to track down the few remaining Nazis, individually responsible for the deaths of thousands, and bringing them to justice.

'But let justice roll on like a river, righteousness like a never-failing stream!'

Amos 5: 24

In February 2004, the Queen awarded Simon Wiesenthal an honorary knighthood to recognize his work.

Simon Wiesenthal with his Medal of Honour, 17 April 2002.

THINK ABOUT IT!

3. In trying to track down former war criminals, do you think that Simon Wiesenthal is letting 'justice roll on like a river'? Explain your answer.

4. Simon Wiesenthal escaped death on several occasions. Was he just lucky or do you think there are other explanations? Give reasons for your answer.

5. a) Make a list of the rights you think everybody should have that Simon Wiesenthal was denied.
   b) Choose one of these rights and explain why you think it is important.

4.4 WHAT DOES THE BIBLE SAY ABOUT WAR?

In this lesson you will:
- explore Bible teachings linked to war and peace
- compare stories and teachings about war.

Prophets People in Judaism who spoke for God and passed on his message to others

● WHAT DOES THE BIBLE SAY ABOUT WAR?

Some of the great heroes in the Old Testament such as King Saul and King David were warriors. However, many of the teachings of the **prophets** looked forward to peace rather than war, and Jesus spoke out against fighting. Is the Bible inconsistent in its attitudes to war?

● THE STORY OF JOSHUA

In the story of Joshua (Joshua 2: 6) Joshua took over from Moses as the leader of the Hebrews. His first task was to lead the Hebrews into the land he believed God had promised them. This land was called Canaan. However, the people of Canaan did not want newcomers to claim the land for themselves. The only option for Joshua was to fight for Canaan and that is precisely what he did, claiming he had God's help and permission.

● THE BATTLE OF JERICHO

The most famous battle Joshua fought for Canaan was at the city of Jericho. Jericho was surrounded by two large walls that made attacking it very difficult. Joshua was not worried about this because he believed he had God on his side. Read below what Joshua planned and what happened.

Battle plan
This is what we are going to do:
1 Two spies go into Jericho to find out more about where their soldiers are. Our spies will be hidden by a woman called Rahab.
2 Camp outside Jericho for seven days. Once, each day for the first six days, we will walk around the city walls. The only noise will be made by our priests blowing trumpets. You must all be quiet.
3 On day seven, prepare for action! We will march around the walls seven times. Then the priests will blow their trumpets and you must all shout as loud as you can. This will make the walls fall down.
4 Go into the city and kill everyone you meet. Do not kill Rahab and her family.
5 If you see anything valuable, take it, and we will give it to God when we have won.

● OTHER VIEWS OF WAR

Although in many places in the Jewish scriptures war is seen as God's way of helping or punishing his people, there are examples of teachings that look forward to a time when war is neither necessary nor acceptable. The prophet Isaiah, who lived over 2500 years ago, foretold that a time would come when people will:

> ❝Beat their swords into ploughshares and their spears into pruning hooks. Nation will not take up sword against nation, nor will they train for war any more.❞
>
> *Isaiah 2: 4*

In the New Testament, Jesus seemed to share this hope and gave advice to people on how to make sure it happened. One of Jesus' best-known teachings advises people to:

> ❝Love your neighbour as yourself.❞
>
> *Luke 10: 27*

Jesus is actually repeating a teaching from the Old Testament (Leviticus 19: 18). However, less well known is his teaching to:

> ❝Love your enemies and pray for those who persecute you.❞
>
> *Mathew 5: 44*

When he was arrested, Jesus refused to fight back and he forgave those who crucified him.

> ❝Father, forgive them, for they do not know what they are doing.❞
>
> *Luke 23: 34*

Ultimately, the Bible is inconsistent in its teachings about war which can lead to confusion about whether war is ever the right course of action.

'The Raising of the Cross' by Gaspar de Crayer. Why did Jesus refuse to fight back to save his own life?

THINK ABOUT IT!

1. Why do you think the Bible is inconsistent in its attitudes to war?

2. Do you think God would help a nation to win a war? Explain your answer.

3. In small groups, prepare a conversation about war between Joshua, Micah and Jesus. Each person should say *at least* three lines.

4. Perform your prepared conversation in front of the class.

In this lesson you will:
- express your own views about pacifism
- explore religious views on peace
- evaluate whether war or peace is more effective in bringing about change.

CONSCIENTIOUS OBJECTORS

In the First World War, around 16,000 Britons refused to fight. They were called conscientious objectors because their conscience would not let them fight. In some cases, their refusal to fight was linked to religious beliefs. In the Second World War, the number of conscientious objectors rose to around 59,000. Before the twentieth century, people who refused to fight in a war ran the serious risk of being executed for cowardice.

Whilst they will not fight, many conscientious objectors are prepared to help their country in a war by volunteering to be involved as ambulance drivers, stretcher-bearers, engineers or cooks for the soldiers. This does not involve having to kill anybody, but they do make a contribution to the war effort.

Lamar: I think that if we are attacked, we must fight fire with fire.

David: If we do, we will give them an excuse to keep fighting.

Lamar: So what should we do, just let them walk all over us?

David: But why have we allowed things to get so bad that we are under threat?

Lamar: Never mind that, you cannot change what has happened.

David: Agreed. But there must be better ways than fighting.

Lamar: If there are, I would like to know what they are!

David: Well, our leaders could try to settle the problems by talking to each other.

Lamar: I would not want to talk to the enemy.

David: But you would be prepared to kill him?

Lamar: Of course. At least I am not a coward.

David: Neither am I. It takes more courage not to fight than it takes to fight.

THINK ABOUT IT!

1. Write what you think the next four lines of Lamar and David's conversation might be.

2. Who do you agree with? Lamar or David? Give reasons for your choice. (You can agree or disagree with both if you want!)

SOME RELIGIOUS TEACHINGS

Some religions seem quite clear about whether to fight or not, whereas others do not. Some wars even appear to be caused by religion. One thing that all religions have in common is the belief that life is very special and should be protected.

- Buddhism is the only religion that does not believe life comes from God, all the others do.

- Killing is considered to be wrong in most circumstances, but for many Christians, Muslims and Jews, it is allowed in war, provided the reason for the war is acceptable. This reason could include a threat to their religion or their country. Some Buddhists would agree in certain circumstances, e.g. self-defence or saving a group of people from a gunman.

- The criteria of the just war and holy war help many religious believers to decide whether or not a war is acceptable. However, there will always be groups of people within each religion that oppose any kind of war (pacifists).

- **Quakers** believe there is never any reason for violence or killing. They have a 'Peace Testimony', which makes it clear that Quakers do not fight in wars.

- Even people without religious beliefs vary in their attitudes towards war. Some humanists refuse to fight because they refuse to kill fellow human beings, whilst others believe they can fight if the consequences of not fighting the war would cause harm to humans. Even though they do not have religious guidelines and rules to follow, they still might have a strict moral code that will help them decide what to do.

Quakers believe there is never any reason for violence or killing as depicted by this tapestry © Quaker Tapestry Scheme.

Stop the War demonstrations in London showed the strength of feeling against the war in Iraq among both religious and non-religious people.

THINK ABOUT IT!

3. In a group of four, spend ten minutes making the religious case either for fighting a war or for being a pacifist. Your teacher will tell you:
   - which point of view you need to concentrate on – fighting or pacifism
   - which religion to base your ideas on.

4. Choose one person to present your ideas in a ten-minute debate.

5. After the debate, use what you have discussed and heard to script a short conversation that might take place between a Christian and a humanist.

In this lesson you will:
- investigate ways in which peace can be achieved using a real life example
- reflect on how you think peace might be achieved.

KEY WORDS

Terrorism Using violent and illegal means to fight for a cause

RELIGION AND WAR

In many people's opinion, religion is one of the main causes of war. They point to conflicts in places like Northern Ireland and Iraq as examples to support their opinion. Clearly, many religious people are eager to argue against this opinion because, with the exception of a holy war, most religions promote peace rather than violence.

CONFLICT IN NORTHERN IRELAND

Towards the end of the twentieth century, thousands of people lost their lives in a long conflict in Northern Ireland. Although there were political reasons for this conflict, opposing sides were often identified as Roman Catholics and Protestants – branches of the Christian Church – as well as republicans and loyalists, which most of them were politically. This identification, whilst a little simplistic, was generally accurate.

During the conflict, explosions and shootings were common and troops from elsewhere in the UK were sent to cities such as Belfast to keep the peace. Inevitably they became targets and hundreds lost their lives trying to keep the opposing sides from fighting.

HOPE FROM TRAGEDY

Not everybody agreed with the separation of Roman Catholics and Protestants, and the violence that went along with it. Pacifist groups were formed to show disapproval. One of these, the Peace People, was started by Betty Williams, Mairead Corrigan and Ciaran McKeown. They were inspired by a tragic incident that took place on 10 August 1976.

Danny Lennon, a young republican who was suspected of being involved in **terrorism**, was being chased in a car by British soldiers. He was shot dead whilst driving and his car ran into an eight-year-old girl and a six-week-old baby boy, killing them instantly.

The community were understandably shocked at the needless deaths, so much so that Betty Williams and Mairead Corrigan were moved to contact their local media to call for an end to the violence.

Betty Williams (left) and Mairead Corrigan (right), leaders of the 'Women for Peace' rally by Protestants and Catholics to end violence in Northern Ireland. Here they are displaying some of the hundreds of telegrams of support they have received from all over the world.

Journalist Ciaran McKeown helped them in this task and the Peace People were born. They held peaceful protests throughout Ireland and did all they could to publicise their activities and help victims of violence. Their campaign of peaceful demonstrations spread to England, Scotland and Wales. They became easily recognizable faces on television and they were keen to get their message across to as many people as they could.

Their Christian beliefs encouraged them to urge people to pray for peace and many Christian leaders, both from the Roman Catholic Church and the Protestant Church, publicly supported their objectives, often in 'joint' declarations or activities. They were awarded the Nobel Peace Prize in 1976 as recognition of their achievement.

In the first six months of the Peace People's existence, the rate of violence fell by 70 per cent, and people started to talk abut peace. However, it took until April 1998 before this was finally achieved. During that time, there was still occasional violence, resulting in loss of life. There was a bomb explosion at a Remembrance Day parade in Enniskillen in 1987 (see page 83), but peace slowly became more of a reality than a hope.

Betty Williams and Mairead Corrigan are Christians, and this was a large motivation for their work. Other Christians also got involved as a result of their faith. Since peace has been achieved in Northern Ireland, Mairead Corrigan has turned her attention to promoting peace in other parts of the world, most notably in Iraq in 2004. Her ideas are summed up in her own words:

> 'If we want to reap the harvest of peace and justice in the future, we will have to sow seeds of non-violence, here and now, in the present.'

A mural declaring 'New Life' in a Belfast suburb following the Irish Peace agreement.

THINK ABOUT IT!

1. Explain carefully why you think Betty Williams and Mairead Corrigan decided to set up 'the Peace People'.

2. *Who's Who?* is a book that gives details about the lives of famous people. Write an entry for Mairead Corrigan. Aim to write around 200 words. You may want to use the Peace People website to find out more information. Access the website by visiting www.heinemann.co.uk/hotlinks, typing in the express code 7266P and clicking on this section.

3. Do you agree with Mairead Corrigan's quote above? Say why or why not.

In this lesson you will:
- investigate the events in the life of the Dalai Lama
- understand the religious motivation of the Dalai Lama
- evaluate Buddhist teachings on non-violence.

KEY WORDS

Dalai Lama Title of the Buddhist leader which means 'Great Ocean'

Exile Forcibly sent to live in a different country

Monasteries Places where monks and nuns live

Many Buddhists believe that one of the main causes of war is people being selfish and wanting things that cannot satisfy them. So fighting in a war only serves what they believe is harmful. Some Buddhists might fight in defence of their nation or their religion, but others believe it is better to die without fighting rather than be forced to harm or kill another human being. This ties in with the idea of ahimsa (non-violence) and the First Precept, which states that Buddhists shall 'not harm any living thing'.

● INVASION

Imagine being chosen to be a religious leader at the age of just two. This is what happened to Lhamo Dhondrub, who was born on 6 July 1935 in north-eastern Tibet. He is now known as Tenzin Gyatso, the **Dalai Lama**. The Dalai Lama is the spiritual and political leader of Buddhists in the mountainous kingdom of Tibet.

In 1950, when the Dalai Lama was fifteen years old, 80,000 Chinese soldiers invaded Tibet. The people of Tibet did not accept the Chinese as their new leaders and respected the Dalai Lama as their leader instead.

As a Buddhist, the Dalai Lama was taught from an early age to find peaceful solutions to problems. So, in 1954, he travelled to China for peace talks. However, the talks failed. In 1959, a group of Tibetans tried to challenge the Chinese leaders and were cruelly defeated. Around 60,000 Tibetan Buddhists were killed. The Dalai Lama feared for his life and, along with around 80,000 of his followers, fled to India where he has lived ever since. Not being allowed to live in your own country is called being sent into **exile**.

Chinese army trucks in Tibet. How would you feel if another country invaded the UK? How would you react?

 THINK ABOUT IT!

1. Explain why many Buddhists refuse to fight in a war.

2. Should a country be allowed to invade and rule another country?

3. Do you think the Dalai Lama was right to flee to India or should he have tried to fight? Give two reasons for him being right and two reasons for him staying to fight.

● LIFE IN EXILE

Despite living in exile, the Dalai Lama is still regarded by many as the leader of Tibetan Buddhism. Back in Tibet, the Chinese have not treated the Buddhists well. 6000 **monasteries** have been destroyed and many spiritually valuable objects (artefacts) and religious books have been destroyed. Despite this, the Dalai Lama has maintained his Buddhist beliefs and never used violence to fight back.

Instead, he has devoted his life to trying to make the rest of the world aware of the situation the Tibetan Buddhists face. He looks forward to the day when he can return to his country to lead his people once again.

In 1989, the Dalai Lama was awarded the Nobel Peace Prize to recognize his non-violent methods in trying to return his country and religion to his people. He puts the teaching of the Buddha into action:

> 'Hatred does not cease by hatred, but only by love; this is the eternal rule.'
>
> *Dhammapada 5*

> 'A man is not a great man because he is a warrior and kills living beings, but because he hurts no living thing. He is in truth called a great man.'
>
> *Dhammapada 270*

The Dalai Lama receiving the Nobel Peace Prize, 1989.

THINK ABOUT IT!

4. Buddhism teaches non-violence. Do you think this is realistic in the twenty-first century? Give reasons for your answer.

WHAT THE TASK IS ALL ABOUT:

1. Write a script for a radio or TV discussion between an interviewer and one of the following:

    a) a World War II veteran soldier who was involved in the D Day landings

    b) a Christian conscientious objector who refused to fight in World War II

    c) a Buddhist who believes in non-violence.

2. If you had to decide whether to fight in a war or not, what and who would influence your decision?

WHAT YOU NEED TO DO TO COMPLETE THE TASK:

- Think carefully about what you are going to write. Plan your answer carefully to make sure you include all the relevant information in your interview script.

- Make sure the interviewer asks the key questions and write the answers from the point of view of a Christian who can justify fighting in WWII, a Christian who cannot justify fighting or a Buddhist who believes in non-violence.

- For the person you choose you need to think carefully about how this person might think and how their beliefs might influence them.

HINTS AND TIPS

- Make sure you include enough detail to show the influence of the person's beliefs.
- Explain the reasons why you hold any opinion you choose to write about.
- Try to show how the person's religious beliefs influence what they think or do.

TO ACHIEVE	YOU WILL NEED TO
Level 3	Show that you understand the importance of religious beliefs and teachings in helping people decide how to act and explain that you know what influences your own decisions.
Level 4	Show that you understand the experiences of a religious person and use your own experience and ideas to show why they did what they did. Explain the religious teachings that influenced how they made their decision. Describe what influences the way you make decisions and act.
Level 5	Explain how the writings and teachings of religions are used to provide answers to questions such as whether to fight or to support a government in going to war or not. Explain your own views about what is involved in doing what a religion teaches.
Level 6	Explain some reasons why religious people have different beliefs about war and use examples to show how religious beliefs relate to teachings and world issues. Give reasons for your own views. Show that you have thought about the challenges and difficulties in putting your values into practice in the world today.

CHAPTER 5

EVIL AND SUFFERING

THE BIGGER PICTURE

In this chapter you will learn about different types of suffering and the reasons for them, including the possible existence of evil. You will also have a chance to explore what can be done to limit suffering.

WHAT?

You will:

- investigate different types of suffering and examples of them
- reflect upon the effect evil and suffering have on people
- understand the religious teachings about evil and suffering
- evaluate religious and non-religious people's responses to evil and suffering.

HOW?

By:

- identifying different types of suffering, as well as the reasons for and responses to suffering
- comparing religious teachings on evil and suffering
- evaluating whether evil causes suffering and whether religion helps to prevent evil and suffering.

WHY?

Because:

- the existence of evil and suffering affects religious belief
- some people believe that evil and suffering prove that God does not exist
- some people believe that religious teachings might help to limit the effect of evil and suffering.

KEY IDEAS

- There are different types of suffering.
- Different things can cause suffering.
- People respond to suffering in different ways.
- You do not have to be religious to care.
- Some Christians and Jews believe that suffering is the result of Adam and Eve disobeying God.
- Suffering makes it difficult for some people to believe in God.
- Buddhism tries to answer questions about suffering.
- Religious people believe they have a duty to help those who suffer and to defeat evil.

KEY WORDS

Natural suffering	Evil
Satan	Ultimate questions
Free will	Heaven
Vicarious	Eternal life
Hell	Four Noble Truths
Buddha	Mara
Dukkha	Tanha
Middle Way	Eightfold path
Five Precepts	Magga
Dhammapada	Karma
Compassion	Zakah

Catholic nuns with the Missionaries of Charity distributing free food to the poor on Christmas Day in Calcutta, 2003. An estimated 20 per cent of Calcutta's 12 million people live in dire poverty and many of them are homeless.

In this lesson you will:
- investigate different types of suffering
- identify and analyse what causes suffering.

KEY WORDS

Natural suffering Pain and suffering caused by nature

Some people seem to go through life quite happily with everything falling into place, whilst some people struggle against suffering possibly caused by illness, accident or what just seems to be sheer bad luck. Why is this? If that question could be answered, everybody would follow the answer and no one would suffer any more. But that is never going to happen. Of course, we can do lots of things to help ourselves. We can work hard and live healthily, but in the end, it is a fact of life that some people will suffer whilst others will not.

NATURAL SUFFERING

Much suffering is nobody's fault. It is caused by nature. We regularly see pictures on television or in newspapers of the effects of earthquakes or floods that destroy homes and kill thousands of people. It can be easy for us to ignore the need of our fellow human beings who are suffering, especially if it is not happening to us or to anybody we know. Some think that because the suffering is nobody's fault, there is no one to blame, so there is nothing we can do. Others are more positive and make an effort to help, but what they can achieve is often limited.

THINK ABOUT IT!

1. Draw a spider diagram with eight legs and 'Suffering' in the middle. On each of the eight legs, write an example of suffering, for example illness.

Natural suffering – a young homeless girl in Meulaboh whose house was destoyed by the tsunami in December 2005.

● SUFFERING CAUSED BY PEOPLE

Unlike **natural suffering**, suffering that is caused by other people should be preventable. However, in many cases, it is not that simple.

There are many people who would like to stop **war**. They believe that the enormous number of lives that are lost during a war makes war wrong. However, people who support war as a way of solving problems point out that sometimes it is necessary. If, for example, one country invades another, they say it is perfectly all right for that country to fight back. Indeed, if they do not fight back, they may be allowing greater suffering to occur to the people in their own country.

🎧 **Suffering caused by people – the terrorist attack on the Twin Towers in September 2001.**

THINK ABOUT IT!

2. Using the spider diagram you made in task 1, decide whether each type of suffering is natural or caused by people and add it to a Venn diagram like the one below. It is possible that some suffering might be both natural and caused by people. If so, put it in the place where the two circles overlap. Are there any types that you cannot classify easily? Why do you think this is?

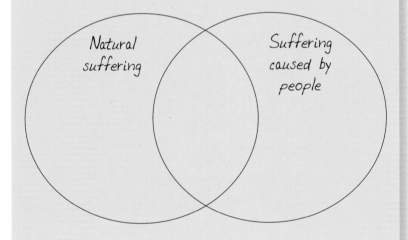

Some people bring suffering upon themselves. Drug addicts are a good example of this. But their suffering is caused by their addiction – they cannot prevent it unless they are able to break the habit and that is sometimes not easy. Their addiction might cause them to turn to crime to get the money they need to buy their drugs. Crimes they commit, like burglary for example, bring suffering on others – the victims of their burglary and upon themselves when they are punished for their crimes.

THINK ABOUT IT!

3. Think of some other types of suffering people bring upon themselves. Explain them and show whether they also cause others to suffer.

4. Write a letter to a friend who is suffering because of their own actions, the actions of others or from natural causes. Give them some advice on what they should do and explain why. You should be sympathetic.

In this lesson you will:
- investigate what evil is
- evaluate the story of the fall in Genesis
- make connections between evil and suffering.

KEY WORDS

Evil Absence of goodness

Satan 'Adversary', a personification of the powers of evil

DOES EVIL EXIST?

In March 1996, a man named Thomas Hamilton walked into a primary school in Dunblane, Scotland. He calmly went to the school's gym and shot fifteen children and their teacher with the rifle he was carrying. He then killed himself. Nobody knows why he did this but the school's head teacher was quoted as saying, '**Evil** visited our school today.'

Whether he was right in blaming evil or not, some people are in no doubt that evil is real and is responsible for many terrible things. For people who believe that evil exists, it is easy to link it to suffering. Evil can and does cause people to suffer. There is no doubt that Thomas Hamilton caused untold suffering to the families of the teacher and children he killed, and that people are still suffering from their memories of his actions. The only doubt is whether he did it because he was influenced by evil or not. We will never know for sure.

Suffering has always existed. In the past, people did not expect to live much beyond the age of 30 and many children died before they reached their first birthday. Food and shelter were scarce. Although people knew the difference between right and wrong, life seemed to have less value. It is little surprise that people were keen to explain why suffering exists and to find out what they could do to prevent it. The answers they came up with were often based on their religion and sometimes involved a power of evil.

Headmaster Ron Taylor holds a press conference at the gates of Dunblane Primary School, 22 March 1996.

THINK ABOUT IT!

1. Do you think the head teacher of Dunblane School was right in saying 'Evil visited our school today'?

2. Why do you think some people look to religion for their answers about suffering?

WHAT CAUSES SUFFERING?

On occasions, the Old Testament Hebrews believed their suffering was caused by God's punishment for their wrongdoing. Several of the prophets from the Old Testament made this point to the people in an attempt to encourage them to follow God properly. However, even though they said God was the cause of their suffering, it was seen as their own fault because they had disobeyed God.

Others blamed suffering on a power of evil. Jews believe that within each individual there is a good and an evil inclination. Bad things happen when we allow the evil inclination to win out. In Christianity, this power of evil became known as the devil or **Satan**. In ancient religion, the tradition grew that good would always defeat evil just as spring always follows winter. Jews and Christians are supported in their belief that evil causes suffering by the story of the Fall in Chapter 3 of Genesis.

ADAM AND EVE

According to this story in Genesis chapter 3, God instructed Adam, the first man, and Eve, the first woman, that they could eat the fruit of all the trees in the garden except for the fruit of the tree that gives knowledge of what is good and what is evil. They were forbidden to eat fruit from this tree.

Adam and Eve lived happily in the Garden of Eden. Some time later, Eve was tempted by a serpent (snake) to disobey God and to eat the forbidden fruit. She then persuaded Adam to do the same. As a punishment, God threw them out of the Garden of Eden. God told Adam that he would have to work hard to earn a living from the land and Eve that she would suffer in childbirth as would all women.

Whether they believe this story is literally true or not, many people associate the snake with the devil. Some people also believe that the suffering that exists in the world today is a result of Adam and Eve falling to the temptation of the devil. In the past, this story was widely accepted as true by Christians and Jews, and some believers in these two religions still believe it today. However, because we now have more knowledge than our ancestors had, most people do not believe that it is literally true. They think the story symbolizes that the devil (a symbol to represent evil) does still have a harmful effect on the world.

🎧 **Does the story of the Fall explain the origins of suffering?**

THINK ABOUT IT!

3. What do you think about the story of Adam and Eve? Is it literally true or is the meaning more important than whether it is literally true?

4. Could this story be 'true' in the sense that it is saying things about human behaviour and the way we see our place in the world? What do you think?

5. Why do you think this story is often called 'the Fall'?

5.3 DOES SUFFERING PROVE THAT THERE IS NO GOD?

In this lesson you will:
- investigate the link between the existence of God and suffering
- explore the belief that suffering proves that God does not exist or does not care for people
- evaluate religious responses to suffering.

KEY WORDS

Ultimate questions
Important questions that religion tries to answer

Free will The idea that human beings have been created with the choice to do either good or evil

● WHY IS THERE SUFFERING?

Many people believe that their religion has the answers to all the difficult **ultimate questions** in life. They believe that religion can answer how the Earth came into being and what happens when we die. Some answers may not be obvious because people cannot know everything about God, but, throughout the centuries, great religious thinkers have come up with answers that seem to satisfy them. It is possible that some of these answers might be wrong.

One of the most difficult of these ultimate questions is: 'Why is there suffering?'

John: You believe in God, don't you?
Alesha: Yes, I do.
John: And you believe God cares for us and wants what is best for us?
Alesha: Er, yes.
John: So how come people suffer?
Alesha: I don't understand your point.
John: Well, if God exists, he would stop people suffering.
Alesha: Don't be silly, of course God exists. Perhaps he chooses not to stop people suffering.
John: You might be right, but if you are, it does not sound as if he cares about us.

THINK ABOUT IT!

1. Continue John and Alesha's conversation with another two lines each about whether God has the power to stop suffering.

2. Do you think God can help people to answer 'ultimate questions'? Give reasons and examples.

Different religions have different answers to the question of suffering. Below are some religious responses to why suffering exists.

- Suffering is God's test to see whether people trust that he cares for them.
- Suffering challenges people and leads them to have a greater understanding of God.
- Suffering allows people a chance to show they care for those who are suffering.
- Suffering is not God's fault, it is humankind's.
- Suffering is caused by evil or the devil and is not God's fault.

> God? What God? Look at me, there can't be a god.

THINK ABOUT IT!

3. Listed above are five possible religious explanations for the existence of suffering. Which explanation makes most sense to you and why? Which makes least sense?

Whichever of these ideas a person believes, there are many who disagree with each of them.

- Some religious people believe there is a difference between the reasons for natural suffering and suffering caused by humans. They believe it is unfair to blame God for natural suffering, even though they may believe that God created the natural world. It is easier to believe that God cannot or might choose not to interfere with suffering caused by humans, but many people who suffer perhaps wish he would.
- Some people doubt that God has enough power to prevent suffering. They say that God cannot have the power to stop suffering, otherwise God would use it to help us.
- If God has the power to stop suffering, and chooses not to use it, the idea of a loving God must be wrong.
- All religious ideas about God imply he is all-powerful and could easily stop people suffering. As people do still suffer, God cannot exist.

● FREE WILL

Many people believe that God gave humans the opportunity to make choices. He does not control people. This is called **free will**. If humans, as a species, choose to behave in a certain way, they have to accept the consequences of these actions. These consequences might be good, but they could also be bad, possibly causing suffering. Whichever they are, people cannot expect God to become involved in them. Perhaps God wants people to learn from bad consequences so they make better choices in the future.

THINK ABOUT IT!

4. Some people argue that God can end suffering but will not. Others argue that God cannot end suffering. What questions would you ask someone who holds one of these beliefs?

5. Explain fully why some people think that suffering is proof that God does not exist.

In this lesson you will:
- apply a Christian teaching about suffering
- show empathy with the reaction of Gordon Wilson to the death of his daughter
- evaluate Gordon Wilson's feelings of forgiveness and mercy
- understand the Christian belief that Jesus suffered on behalf of others (vicariously).

KEY WORDS

Heaven Spiritual home of God

Vicarious Experiencing something on behalf of someone else e.g. suffering

Eternal life Belief in living forever

Hell Spiritual home of the Devil

RESPONDING TO NATURAL SUFFERING

Most Christians believe that natural suffering is not caused by God, even though they believe he created the world. Below are two Christian responses to natural suffering. What do you think?

> Droughts and floods would not be such a problem if richer countries helped the poorer countries to cope better, and if they looked after the environment better.

Kim

How should a Christian respond to the suffering of this Ethiopian woman and her child.

> Volcanoes and earthquakes are necessary for the world to survive. God does not make people choose to live near volcanoes or build cities in places where earthquakes are likely to happen.

Luke

WHAT DID JESUS SAY?

> 'Do not store up for yourselves treasures on Earth…But store up for yourselves treasures in **heaven**…For where your treasure is, there your heart will be also.'
>
> *Matthew 6: 19–21*

Many Christians argue that following Jesus' teachings and sharing what they have helps those who suffer. They believe that God has shown people through the Bible how to prevent suffering, but many choose to ignore it.

THINK ABOUT IT!

1. Explain how following the teaching of the quote above might help to reduce suffering.

RESPONDING TO SUFFERING CAUSED BY HUMANS

Some suffering is the result of the evil that people have chosen to do. However, hatred does not have to be met with further hatred. An example of someone who put this belief into practice is Gordon Wilson.

'I BEAR NO GRUDGE'

On 8 November 1987, a bomb exploded in Enniskillen in Northern Ireland amongst a crowd of people who had gathered for a Remembrance Day service. Marie Wilson, a nurse, was one of the eleven people who were killed by the bomb. That same evening, Marie's father, Gordon Wilson, who himself was injured in the blast, appeared on television to give his reaction to his daughter being murdered in this way. Instead of swearing revenge, he said:

'I have lost my daughter and we shall miss her, but I bear no ill will. I bear no grudge. Dirty sort of talk is not going to bring her back to life. I shall pray for those people tonight and every night.'

THINK ABOUT IT!

2. What do you think about Gordon Wilson's reaction to his daughter's killers? Explain your answer.

WHAT IS THE POINT OF SUFFERING?

- For many Christians, the idea of **vicarious** suffering is very important. Vicarious suffering is when someone chooses to suffer for and on behalf of others. Many Christians believe that this is what happened when Jesus died on the cross. He dealt with the consequences of the sin that people had done.

- Jesus' death is also important to many Christians because they believe that he was the Son of God, God in human flesh, and therefore God experienced suffering and death first hand.

- Many Christians also believe that there is a heaven, a place of paradise and that God gives people **eternal life**. Their belief in life after death might help them to cope with suffering, as they can look forward to things being better after death. Many Christians also believe in a **hell**, where those who have committed evil will be dealt with by the devil.

Can you think of anyone other than Jesus who has suffered on behalf of others?

THINK ABOUT IT!

3. Explain how Jesus' death helps Christians gain comfort in times of suffering.

4. Do you agree with any of the suggested reasons for suffering on these pages? If so, why? If not, what do you think is the point of suffering?

In this lesson you will:
- analyze the Buddhist teaching of the Four Noble Truths
- express personal beliefs and ideas about these teachings.

Some people seem to spend a lot of time moaning or complaining. Often there is a good reason for this, sometimes there may not be. They almost always blame everybody but themselves, and do not always choose the right person to blame!

Siddhartha Gautama witnessed suffering in his life. However, he was not interested in blaming other people for this. Instead he set about finding the root cause of suffering.

He decided to sit in meditation under the Bodhi Tree at Bodh Gaya in order to find out the answer to the question of why people suffer dissatisfaction and stress. While he was meditating, the devil (in Buddhism called **Mara**) tempted him and tried to distract him from his thoughts. But Siddhartha resisted and reached a state of Enlightenment, at which point he became the Buddha. In this Enlightened state, he realized the nature of human desire and how this can lead to suffering.

THE FOUR NOBLE TRUTHS

The Buddha set out his teaching on suffering in the **Four Noble Truths**.

1 There is **dukkha** everywhere, nothing is perfect (a statement of fact). Life is unsatisfactory because there is suffering.

2 Dukkha is caused by people's desiring things (the cause): desire is called **tanha**. This is an attempt to explain what causes suffering. Someone's desire can lead to suffering for themselves and to others.

3 Removing desire will remove dissatisfaction and suffering (the solution). If something creates a problem, removing it should solve the problem.

4 Desire, dissatisfaction and suffering can be removed by following the **Middle Way**, or **magga**, of the **Eightfold Path** (the advice).

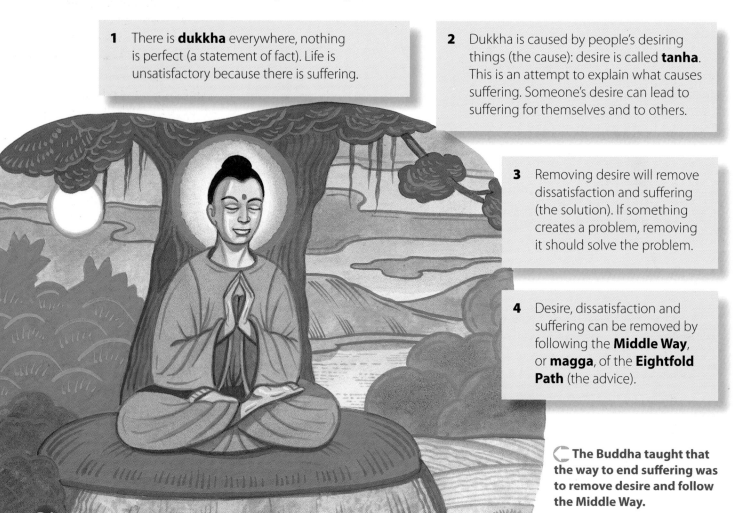

The Buddha taught that the way to end suffering was to remove desire and follow the Middle Way.

The fourth Noble Truth shows the Buddha's Enlightened state. Steps 1–3 are very logical, whereas step 4 offers a way of making sure people try to resist their desire, which will in turn free them from dissatisfaction and suffering.

The rest of the Buddha's teaching is designed to give advice on how to achieve this freedom from desire and suffering.

Something is wrong with this person, there must be a cause. I will find out the cause, cure him and advise him on how to live a healthier life in the future.

KEY WORDS

Buddha Title given to Siddhartha Gautama which means the 'Awakened or Enlightened One'

Mara Personification of evil in Buddhism

Four Noble Truths Fundamental Buddhist teaching about the causes of suffering and how to remove it from our lives

Dukkha dissatisfaction with life. Buddhists believe that this can lead to suffering

Tanha Buddhist idea of craving or desire

Middle Way The Buddhist Eightfold Path which creates a balance between the extremes of pain, self-denial, pleasure and self-indulgence

Eightfold path Buddhist teaching on the Middle Way which helps Buddhists to attain Nirvana

Magga the path to release from suffering

THINK ABOUT IT!

1. Copy these four statements and add your own ideas in the spaces.

   a) Dukkha is caused by _____.

   b) If we remove _____ we will remove suffering.

   c) _____ and therefore suffering can be removed by

   following _____.

2. Explain how the doctor's logic in the picture above matches the Four Noble Truths.

3. Explain what 'dukkha', 'tanha' and 'magga' mean.

4. Do you agree that the Four Noble Truths are sensible and logical? Explain your answer.

In this lesson you will:
- reflect on Buddhist teaching in the Eightfold Path and the Five Precepts
- evaluate whether Buddhist teaching reduces suffering
- express your personal ideas about the Eightfold Path and the Five Precepts.

KEY WORDS

Five Precepts Buddhist guidelines about behaving well

Karma A teaching which states that all actions will influence future lives

Dhammapada A Buddhist Holy Book

● THE EIGHTFOLD PATH

Some people try to live their lives by the philosophy 'everything in moderation'. This means they will try most things, but not to any extreme. For example, they might drink alcohol, but not so much that they get drunk, or if they buy luxuries, they will not overspend. Doing everything in moderation helps them to live their lives comfortably without causing problems for themselves or others.

The Middle Way in Buddhism, however, is different and it is explained in the Eightfold Path. Buddhists believe that by following the Eightfold Path they can find a way to end suffering.

The Eightfold Path is made up of eight elements:

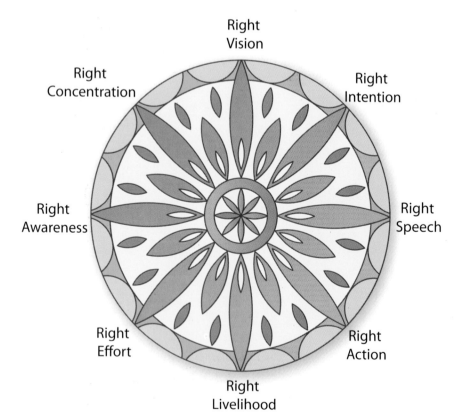

Right Vision
Right Intention
Right Speech
Right Action
Right Livelihood
Right Effort
Right Awareness
Right Concentration

However, the Eightfold Path is only helpful if it is followed and understood properly, otherwise a person could do something that goes against Buddhist teaching and use the excuse that it was right action because he thought it was the right thing to do. This could even cause themselves or other people to suffer – the opposite of what the Eightfold Path intends to happen. To be sure that their interpretation is right, they have to understand the teaching of the Buddha, so the first step on the path (right understanding) is to understand the Four Noble Truths and Eightfold Path correctly as the Buddha intended.

🎧 **The symbol of the Eightfold Path is a wheel with eight spokes. The wheel helps to remind Buddhists of the circle of life.**

THINK ABOUT IT!

1. If the Eightfold Path became the Ninefold Path, what would you like the ninth step to be? Explain why. Remember to think about how your step could help people lead a better life and reduce suffering.

THE FIVE PRECEPTS

The Buddha offered more advice on how to live a good life that avoided causing suffering. This advice to followers is contained within the **Five Precepts**.

1. Avoid taking life and harming living beings.
2. Avoid taking what is not given and is not one's own.
3. Avoid sexual activity that does not include love, care and commitment.
4. Avoid telling lies.
5. Avoid intoxicating drinks and drugs.

These give more specific guidance than the Eightfold Path and if they are followed, they cover much of what the Eightfold Path requires of Buddhists, thereby limiting suffering. They will also help to prevent incorrect interpretations of what is required by the Eightfold Path, furthering the aim of reducing suffering.

THINK ABOUT IT!

2. Do you think the Eightfold Path and the Five Precepts stop people from suffering? Explain your answer.

SO WHY DO PEOPLE SUFFER?

Buddhists believe that some people suffer due to bad actions (**karma**) in their previous life. They believe that if they have followed religious teachings well in their previous life, they might suffer less in this life.

However, suffering can also be caused by what a person does in their present life. The first verse of the **Dhammapada** (a Buddhist holy book) states:

'If a man speaks or acts with an impure mind, suffering follows him as the wheel of the cart follows the beast that draws the cart.'

Buddhists believe that there are three things that poison life by causing suffering. These are:
- ignorance (mainly of the Buddha's teachings)
- greed (wanting what will not satisfy you)
- selfishness (putting your own desires before other people).

Removing these things from our life by following the Eightfold Path and the Five Precepts would go a long way to help to stop suffering.

THINK ABOUT IT!

3. Explain what you think the first verse of the Dhammapada means.

4. Do you agree that following religious teaching stops people from suffering? Explain your answer.

5.7 WHAT CAN BE DONE ABOUT EVIL AND SUFFERING?

In this lesson you will:
- analyze what can be done to limit evil and suffering
- reflect on religious and non-religious ideas.

KEY WORDS

Zakah Islamic practice of giving 2.5 per cent of savings to those in need

Compassion Sympathy for people in need

SUFFERING

For many people in the world, suffering is a daily issue. The only way to survive is to rely on other people. Anybody who is in hospital, for instance, is dependent on the doctors and nurses to make sure they are comfortable and hopefully recover from whatever is wrong with them.

OVERCOMING SUFFERING IN DEVELOPING COUNTRIES

People in developing countries are often dependent on the help of others. If their crops fail because of drought or floods, they rely on others to help them. If their home is blown away in a tropical storm or is destroyed by an earthquake, they have no insurance policy to pay for a new home. They rely on people who are inspired to do good either because they think God wants them to or because they think it is the 'right and human' thing to do.

This woman survived an earthquake, but everything that she owns has been destroyed. What could be done to ease her suffering?

THINK ABOUT IT!

1. Explain what you think it feels like to depend on other people for help.

2. What causes people in developing countries to rely on other people to help them?

RELIGIOUS RESPONSES

All religions encourage believers to take the responsibility of doing something to help.

- Christians believe that Jesus told a parable to encourage people to help others. It is called the Parable of the Good Samaritan (Luke 10: 25–37). Jews also share the belief that God wants us to love our neighbour.
- Muslims have to give a donation (**zakah**) to charity every year as part of their religion.

COMIC RELIEF – RED NOSE DAY

Giving money to charity or even working for a charity, however, is not just a religious idea. Most people do this as a response to seeing other human beings suffer.

On Christmas Day in 1985, BBC1 broadcast a report from a refugee camp in Sudan at the height of a famine which claimed the lives of millions of people across the continent of Africa. This report was compiled and presented by some well known British comedians and launched 'Comic Relief' – a charity which helps people in both Africa and Britain.

The charity came to the attention of the British public in 1988 when they held the first Red Nose Day. This raised around £15 million. There have now been ten Red Nose Days, raising a total of over £350 million. This money has supported the people of Africa in the following ways:

- helped people rebuild their communities
- educated people about HIV and Aids – a disease which kills many thousands every year
- immunised children against diseases
- given women the chance to learn how to read.

In Britain, it has supported the disabled, given children real opportunities to achieve a good start in life and helped victims of all ages who were suffering from abuse.

Most people are capable of showing **compassion**, with or without the help of religion. The celebrities who started Comic Relief do not claim any special religious motivation for their actions, just a desire to help their fellow human beings. However, there is no doubt that religious believers do a lot to help people who suffer and also to try to make sure that evil does not spread.

🎧 **Through the Parable of the Good Samaritan Jesus encouraged his followers to help those in need.**

THINK ABOUT IT!

3. According to Jesus, why should Christians help others?

4. What do you think 'compassion' means? Think of other words that are connected with the word compassion and write them down.

What the task is all about:

Choose one of these four tasks. Your teacher might choose one for you.

1. Script a conversation between a person who is suffering and a believer of one of the religions you have studied. Include comments that show the beliefs of the religious person about why suffering exists, and how and why they think they should offer help.

2. Make a presentation about suffering and the problems it causes to religious believers. Include some ideas to explain religious beliefs about responding to suffering. You could present your work using ICT. Save or print it so your teacher can mark it.

3. Make a list of questions you would like to ask a religious believer about problems with and responses to suffering. Write the answers you would expect a religious believer to give to your questions.

4. Write a newspaper article of around 300 words. Your headline is: 'Religious person explains all about suffering'.

What you need to do to complete the task:

- Whichever task you choose, you should think carefully before you write anything. You may find it easier if you make some brief notes before you start, but do not take too long over this.
- Remember that you have to include some religious teachings.
- If you give opinions in an answer, make sure you include some reasons for them, including religious ones.

Hints and tips

- Make sure you include enough detail to answer your question in full.
- When you are asked for an opinion, you should give your reasons as well.
- Once you have given your reasons, try to think of a different opinion from your own and give reasons for that different opinion as well.
- Try to show how the beliefs of a religion affect what a religious person thinks or does.

TO ACHIEVE	YOU WILL NEED TO
Level 3	Show that you understand that religions have different explanations about the reasons for suffering and ask questions about the ways in which beliefs about why people suffer influence people's lives.
Level 4	Compare the beliefs of different religions about suffering and describe how these beliefs affect people's lives.
Level 5	Show how the religions you have studied use different teachings, stories and experiences to provide answers to the difficult question of why people suffer. Give your own views on how religions have tried to answer this challenging question.
Level 6	Think about the question of suffering in greater depth so that you can explain why people from different religions and traditions give different answers to this question. Explain why the question of suffering poses particular challenges for religious people living in the world today.

THE ENVIRONMENT

THE BIGGER PICTURE

In this chapter you will examine ways in which religions and worldviews express beliefs about the natural world in which we live. Many people believe that the way humans exploit the environment is the greatest threat to the future of the planet. It is therefore important to understand the arguments involved in debates about the environment. It may seem to you that individuals cannot make a difference to something as big as the future of the planet. Many people would argue, however, that unless everyone is prepared to take responsibility for the world, change will not happen.

WHAT?

You will:

- examine the effect that humans have had on the natural world in which they live
- investigate different reasons for arguing that humans should take responsibility for the environment
- evaluate the influence of religious and non-religious beliefs on attitudes to caring for the environment.

HOW?

By:

- collecting information about damaging changes to the environment
- examining religious and non-religious beliefs about human responsibility for the environment
- making links between beliefs about and action towards the world.

WHY?

Because:

- in order to play an active part in the world in which we live – and have some influence on its future – we need to understand debates about the environment
- to appreciate the arguments, we need to understand the ways in which beliefs affect actions
- if we can make well-informed decisions, we might then be able to act in a way that has a positive effect on the future of our planet.

KEY IDEAS

- Environmental damage is believed by many people to be the greatest threat to the planet and to human survival.
- Religious and non-religious teachings about the world and humans' place in it affect attitudes towards caring for the environment.
- Religious and ethical beliefs have inspired some people to take action in order to save the environment.
- Environmental issues mean that we need to think about our attitude to the world and consider our sense of responsibility to it.

KEY WORDS

Environment	Pollution
Gaia hypothesis	Industrialized
Fossil fuels	Ozone layer
Eco-systems	Ecological
Monotheistic	Atman
Vegans	Ahimsa
Ecology	Sewa
Creation	Dominion
Stewardship	Interdependence
Indigenous	Reservations
Pagan	Global warming
Carbon neutral	Deforestation
Interfaith dialogue	Biodegrade

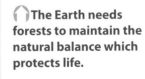
The Earth needs forests to maintain the natural balance which protects life.

Humans have caused so much destruction through greed and waste that many people believe environmental damage is the greatest threat facing our planet. Do you agree?

In this lesson you will:
- examine information about the ecological damage done to the planet
- reflect on the evidence for believing that environmental issues are of great importance for the future of the world
- process information about the environmental damage done to the planet.

• WHAT A MESS!

If we imagine the life of planet Earth to be one day, according to most scientists, humans would only have been on it for a few seconds! Yet, in that brief time, they have managed to cause so much damage that the planet may never recover.

So, what is the problem? 'The **environment**' means the overall condition needed to ensure the growth and survival of living things. The development of modern society has caused so much **pollution** that it is threatening the environment.

In order for life to exist on Earth, there has to be a very delicate balance of different gases and chemicals. Some people believe that this in itself is a miracle. In 1969, a scientist, James Lovelock, put forward the remarkable theory that the Earth itself is a living organism that would protect itself if necessary – which might mean getting rid of the human race! He called this the **Gaia hypothesis**, named after an ancient Earth goddess. Lovelock's argument that the planet is a living being has changed many people's beliefs about the environment and humans' place in it.

KEY WORDS

Environment The surroundings in which a person, animal or plant lives, often taken to mean the natural world

Pollution Harmful waste materials released into the environment

Gaia hypothesis The idea that the Earth is a living organism, and will defend itself even against human beings

Industrialized The term used to describe a country or area which has developed many companies and factories

Fossil fuels Fuels such as petrol, coal or natural gas which consist of the remains of organisms preserved in rocks in the Earth's crust

Ozone layer The layer of gas that protects the Earth from the sun's harmful rays

Eco-systems A system formed by the ways in which living beings fit into their physical environment

Ecological Study of the relationships between living beings and their environments, often used to describe practices which help the environment

THINK ABOUT IT!

1. Discuss the arguments for and against believing that the Earth is 'alive'. What difference would it make to our beliefs about the importance of humans if Lovelock were right?

CLIMATE CHANGE

Modern, **industrialized** living uses huge amounts of energy. Energy is usually generated by **fossil fuels** such as coal or oil.	When these are used, for instance by driving cars or making electricity, they produce carbon dioxide.	So much carbon dioxide is released into the atmosphere that a layer is forming around the Earth, trapping in the warmth and creating a 'greenhouse effect'.	As a result, the Earth's temperature is rising and ice caps are melting, causing destructive changes in the climate.	The trees and plants that could balance this out (because they use carbon dioxide to create oxygen) are being destroyed.

At the same time, other machines, such as fridges and aerosols, produce CFC gases, which damage the planet's **ozone layer**, removing protection from the harmful rays of the sun.

IS TIME RUNNING OUT?

In 2005, scientists produced a report from global research organized by the World Bank. In it they said that two-thirds of the world's **eco-systems** were already badly damaged or destroyed, making it doubtful that the planet would be able to sustain life in the future.

In the same year, some **environmentalists** argued that humanity only had about ten years to make a drastic change to the way they treated the environment before it would be too late to turn back the destruction they had caused.

Not everyone agrees with this view. Some American scientists question whether climate change is the result of human-made pollution and suggest that it is due to natural patterns of weather.

The followers of some religions also question whether we should consider **ecological** issues to be important. Some Christians, for instance, trust that God has given the world to humans for their use. They also believe in Bible passages that foretell the end of the world and describe terrible, natural disasters as the beginning of this time. Such Christians argue that it is more important to try and convert people to save them from this divine judgement rather than concentrate on saving nature. Not all Christians would agree with them, however. We will be looking at more religious approaches to the environment in the following lessons.

 **Because of climate change, destruction of the environment and pollution, scientists predict that by 2025 two-thirds of the world's population will be living in areas without enough water.**

THINK ABOUT IT!

2. Use the information in this chapter to make a spider diagram showing the dangers facing the planet. Place a picture of planet Earth in the centre of the page and draw lines to sentences about the environmental threats to the world. Make sure that you organize the information to show as much evidence as possible, including the arguments against as well as the evidence for the view that environmental damage is the most serious threat to the world.

6.2 RELIGIONS AND THE ENVIRONMENT

In this lesson you will:
- investigate the ways in which several world religions teach respect for nature
- make connections between religious worldviews and attitudes to the environment.

KEY WORDS

Monotheistic Belief that there is only one God

Atman The Hindu belief in the soul, which is part of every living being

Vegans People who only eat fruit, vegetables and grain, no meat, fish or dairy produce

Ahimsa Non-violence, respect for life

Ecology Study of the way in which different factors work together to make life possible

Sewa Sikh requirement to help others

All the major world religions have something to say about how we should treat the world around us.

'The Earth is the Lord's, and everything in it'

Psalm 24: 1

Judaism is a **monotheistic** religion. Jews believe that God created the world and that humans should look after it. There are many teachings in Jewish writings about the importance of taking care of the environment.

- There are laws to protect the countryside, even in times of war:

'When you lay siege to a city for a long time, fighting against it to capture it, do not destroy its trees by putting an axe to them, because you can eat their fruit. Do not cut them down. Are the trees of the field people, that you should besiege them?'

Deuteronomy 20: 19

- Some of the most important religious festivals in Judaism also mark the change of the seasons. Sukkot, for instance, remembers a time in the history of the Jews when they were wandering in the wilderness after escaping from slavery in Egypt. At the same time, however, it is also a Harvest festival.
- In addition to this, Judaism celebrates a New Year for trees! The festival of Tu B'Shvat takes place around February (this would be the beginning of spring in Israel). It is the custom at this time to eat a seasonal fruit that you have not yet tasted that year and give a special blessing to the trees. Jews should not cut down a tree without planting a new one and they should not pick the fruit from a new tree for three years to allow it to establish itself.

Ultra orthodox Jews pray for the fruit on the table during a traditional Jewish holiday known as Tu B'Shvat. This Jewish celebration is a time to appreciate the world.

THINK ABOUT IT!

1. Create a festival to mark the New Year for another part of the natural world, for example an animal or flower. What would you choose and why? What customs would you have to celebrate this?

● ALL LIFE IS SACRED

Some people believe that not only is the Earth created by God, but that it is part of the divine. Hinduism teaches us that there is an ultimate reality (**Brahman**) which exists everywhere. It is eternal, unlike material things, which are created, endure for some time and are eventually destroyed. Brahman, spirit, is the source of this temporary world.

According to Hindu belief, every creature is conscious due to the presence of the **atman**, the soul. This soul is also Brahman and a part of God (the supreme Brahman). For this reason, Hinduism teaches great respect for life, including fish, plants & trees, insects, birds and animals. A related principle is **ahimsa**, non-violence. Many Hindus practice ahimsa by being vegetarians or **vegans**.

Jain monks often wear masks over their mouths – not to protect themselves, but to make sure that they do not harm any small flies. They also use a broom to sweep the ground as they walk to avoid treading on any insects.

I think that Buddhism has a lot to say about **ecology** and the environment. The Buddha taught us that all beings are connected and that all life should be respected. We learn how to have compassion for everything that feels. One of the things we should try to have is 'right livelihood'. This means that you should not earn your money by doing anything that harms others. I think that if everyone followed this teaching, the future of the planet would be much safer.

Dhiman

THINK ABOUT IT!

2. Summarize the ideas in this lesson by producing a concept map. Place the planet Earth in the centre of the page and draw lines to the religions and beliefs, writing a sentence to explain the connection. Then draw more lines between the different religions and beliefs to highlight any similarities you can see.

As a Sikh, my most important duty is **sewa**, taking care of others. This includes looking after the environment. The Guru Granth Sahib teaches that God created everything and that everything is a part of God so is of equal importance. We learn stories about the gurus, which show how they taught us to look after the natural world. In an important prayer called the Japji, we say: 'Air is the Guru, water the Father, Earth the mighty Mother of all.'

Ranjit

In this lesson you will:
- evaluate beliefs about the importance of human beings in the world
- express your own opinions about whether humans have a right to control the world.

THINK ABOUT IT!

1. Imagine your journey to school; perhaps you walk or maybe you are driven. Along the way you see lots of different things such as trees, buildings and cars. Separate the things that you see into two columns under the headings 'Natural' and 'Human-made'. Is one column easier to fill than the other, or are they roughly equal? What does this tell you about the environment you live in?

It is often easy to think of humans as the most important creatures on the planet. After all, humans make the biggest impact on the world around us, changing landscapes and the lives of plants and animals according to our needs. Imagine how different the world that we live in today would look without the changes that have been made by human beings.

For many religious people there are two key ideas that help to shape their beliefs about the place of human beings in the world: these ideas are known as **creation** and **dominion**.

Throughout history, the idea that humans are very important has been backed up in stories about creation. Many religions teach that a God or gods created the world and human beings are central to how and why the world was created.

The Jewish, Christian and Islamic traditions share two creation stories:

- the seven-day account of creation
- the story of Adam and Eve.

Many of the ideas about human rights and responsibilities that people believe today are found in those stories. Below is a quote from the book of Genesis:

> ‘God blessed them [Adam and Eve] and said to them, "Be fruitful and increase in number; fill the Earth and subdue it. Rule over the fish of the sea and the birds of the air and over every living creature that moves on the ground."
>
> Then God said, "I give you every seed-bearing plant on the face of the whole Earth and every tree that has fruit with seed in it. They will be yours for food. And to all the beasts of the Earth and birds of the air and all the creatures that move on the ground – everything that has the breath of life in it – I give every green plant for food."’
>
> *Genesis 1: 28–30*

THINK ABOUT IT!

2. The quote from Genesis can be understood in many different ways. Below are three ideas that people have taken from this passage. Read through the quote again and for each idea provide supporting evidence from the quote.
   - Humans should control the whole world
   - Animals all have a special place in the world
   - Humans should be vegetarian

WHAT IS DOMINION?

The word 'dominion' is often used when talking about humankind's place within God's creation. It is a word that can mean control, or authority, and many creation stories focus on the idea that God has given human beings dominion over the world.

The belief that God has put people in charge of the planet has been used in different ways over thousands of years.

- Some people understand dominion to mean that humans are not just very important, but are more important than all other life on Earth. This has sometimes been used to justify destructive actions. For example, if humans 'need' a road or shopping centre, some people would argue that it is acceptable to destroy land that might be home to many different animals in order to build these things.

- Others think of dominion as the responsibility to look after God's world. Humans are in charge because they are capable of making sure that all God's creations are cared for. Many Jewish and Christian people have argued that being a 'good' human involves caring for all forms of life, not just humanity: Proverbs 12: 10 states that, 'a righteous man cares for the needs of his animals'.

THINK ABOUT IT!

3. You are going to prepare to enter the debate. The motion is: 'Humans can do whatever they want to the world.' You will need to write down:
   - ideas that support this statement
   - ideas that oppose this statement.

4. When you have reached a decision about which side of the debate you will argue, you will need:
   - quotes and/or evidence in support of your argument
   - ideas, quotes and/or evidence that highlight the problems of the opposite argument.

   Remember, your aim is to convince those listening that your opinion is the best!

According to some people, humans are in charge of the earth and are more important than animals. Do you agree?

6.4 ARE YOU A STEWARD?

In this lesson you will:
- investigate the responsibilities of 'stewardship'
- reflect upon the consequences of ignoring those responsibilities.

KEY WORDS

Stewardship Looking after something so it can be passed on to the next generation

Interdependence The idea that all forms of life depend upon each other

WHO OWNS THE WORLD?

Many people would claim to 'own' parts of the world; for example, the home you live in and the ground it is built on 'belong' to somebody. Do the people who own land have the right to do whatever they like with it, regardless of how that might affect others, or should their actions be controlled?

THINK ABOUT IT!

1. Below is a selection of seven common answers to the question: 'Who owns the world?' Choose three and for each one suggest how somebody could back up that answer.
   - Everybody
   - God
   - Governments
   - Royalty
   - The richest people
   - Nobody
   - The first people to claim it

WHAT IS A STEWARD?

In the last lesson you discussed ideas about creation and dominion. In the debate about how humans should treat the world, some of you might have raised the idea that being in control of the world, or a part of it, means that we are responsible for taking good care of it. This idea is known as **stewardship**. A steward can be thought of as a caretaker or guardian. Many religious and non-religious people would say that humans are stewards of God's creation.

A MUSLIM VIEW

Many Muslims believe that humans have a special responsibility given to them by Allah to act as guardians of the planet. In Arabic, the language that the Muslim holy book the Qur'an is written in, the word 'guardian' is often translated as 'khalifa'. In the Qur'an it is written:

> 'It is Allah who has made you khalifas of the Earth.'
>
> *Surah 6: 165*

In the Hadith, the sayings of the Prophet Muhammad, Muslims can find more direction about what being a khalifa or steward involves. For example:

> 'The Earth is green and beautiful and Allah has made you His stewards over it.'
>
> *The Hadith*

This saying has been used to support the idea that destruction of the natural world is wrong – the Earth that humans must take care of is green and beautiful.

Do you think that the Prime Minister should take the lead in caring for the environment? If so how and why might he/she do this?

Over the course of human history hunting has been important. Today, many Muslims believe that hunting is only acceptable if other food is not readily available. Hunting as a form of entertainment is sometimes referred to as a 'blood sport'. The Hadith is quite clear about the issue of 'blood sports'.

> ❝If someone kills a sparrow for sport, then that sparrow will call out on the Day of Judgement, "O Lord! That person killed me for nothing! He did not kill me for any useful purpose!"❞
>
> *The Hadith*

This quote is often used to argue that hunting animals for sport is wrong and that those who abuse the world that they are entrusted to protect will have to explain themselves to God.

● INDEPENDENT OR INTERDEPENDENT?

Some people would say that humans are part of a fine balance of life. This means that we are not separate from the natural world and if we take care of the environment, it will look after us.

Below is a Jewish story that aims to explain the idea of **interdependence**. It shows that we share the world and we should avoid selfish actions that might damage our environment.

THINK ABOUT IT!

2. What might being a 'steward of the Earth' involve? Below are four sub-headings: choose at least two and under each one record a list of things that stewards should try to prevent and things that stewards should try to encourage.
- The environment
- Technology and production
- Human beings
- Other living creatures

3. Would it be possible to be a steward if you only focused on one of the four areas above or would that mean that one type of stewardship became more important than another?

4. The Jewish story in the box below shows that ideas about stewardship are not new, they have been around for thousands of years. Your task is to update this story for the twenty-first century. You will need to think of symbols for the world (in the story this is the boat), the stewards (the people in the boat), the destructive steward (the one with the saw). Keep the original story in mind. You might like to plan a different outcome for your story.

Four people had saved up enough money to buy a beautiful boat; they each put up a quarter of the boat's cost. One fine day, they agreed to take their boat out onto the water. In the middle of the sea, while three of the four people were relaxing, the fourth produced a saw from a bag and began to cut a hole in the boat.

'What are you doing?' cried the other three. 'You'll sink the boat!'

'Nonsense,' replied the fourth. 'This is my quarter of the boat and I'll do what I want with it.'

Eventually the whole boat sank.

In this lesson you will:
- examine beliefs that nature is sacred
- evaluate the effects of beliefs on people's attitudes to the environment
- communicate your ideas about religious attitudes to the environment.

KEY WORDS

Indigenous The original or native inhabitants of a place

Reservations Areas where Native Americans were forced to live after they had been conquered by the white settlers, often situated in harsh land which was difficult to live in

Pagan Follower of a religion, based on ancient traditions, which teaches that nature is sacred

Many **indigenous** peoples, such as the Native Americans and the Australian Aborigines, hold religious beliefs that honour the Earth as sacred and understand humans to be part of nature. Most of these people were conquered by white settlers who took away their land. These beliefs have survived, however, and many modern native people are starting to reclaim their ancient traditions.

When white European settlers travelled to the USA, most of them were Christians who believed that God had given them this 'new' land to use for themselves. This is sometimes called dominion (see pages 98–9). They understood land to be property that they could possess and build fences around. They also believed that it was part of God's plan to tame the wilderness and civilize the 'wild' native peoples who lived in it.

By the end of the nineteenth century, the white settlers had killed most of the Native Americans, destroyed the buffalo herds on which they depended and taken the land as their own. They forced the few remaining members of native tribes to live on **reservations**, in harsh, difficult land, far away from the areas they had lived in for generations.

In the mid-1850s, the US government wanted to buy the lands of some of the native people they had defeated. The respected and peaceful leader of the Native Americans, Chief Seattle, gave a speech in his own language, saying that it was not possible to 'own' the Earth because it was living and sacred. He explained the religious beliefs of his people: that humans were part of nature, they were not made to rule over it. Here are some extracts from an English translation of what he said.

> 'The Earth does not belong to us. We belong to the Earth.'
>
> *Words from the speech of Chief Seattle*

Native Americans are often portrayed as 'savages' in films, but they have cultures and spiritualities which respect and care for all forms of life.

'My mother told me
Every part of the Earth is sacred to our people.
My father said to me
We are part of the Earth and it is part of us.
The perfumed flowers are our sisters
The bear, the deer, the great eagle, these are our brothers.
My ancestors said to me, this we know:
We did not weave the web of life,
We are merely a strand in it.
What we do to the web, we do to ourselves.'

Words from the speech of Chief Seattle

'I am the beauty of the green Earth and the white moon among the stars and the mysteries of the waters. I am the soul of nature that gives life to the universe. From Me all things proceed and to Me they must return.'

The Charge of the Goddess

🎧 **Modern Pagans celebrate festivals that mark the change of the seasons in places they believe were sacred sites centuries before Christianity came to Europe.**

THINK ABOUT IT!

1. Explain in your own words what you think the last three lines of the second extract from Chief Seattle's speech mean.

Several Native American leaders warned that if the white settlers carried on destroying the natural world, they would eventually harm themselves. Some people think that those predictions are now proving to be true – see pages 94–5.

THINK ABOUT IT!

2. As a group, decide what you think are the most important questions raised by the information here. It could be something like:
   ● has Christianity done more harm than good to the world?
   ● has modern progress been a good thing?
   ● should we try to follow the example of Pagan religions?
   ● are the beliefs of native spiritualities primitive and superstitious?
   When you have decided which question to debate, give your opinions but only speak when you can say 'I agree/disagree with … because …'

● WHAT IS PAGANISM?

Native or indigenous spiritualities are often described as '**Pagan**', coming from the Latin word paganus, which means 'person living on the land'. Today, some people in western industrialized countries agree with Chief Seattle that they are losing their sense of connection with the natural world. These people sometimes claim to be modern Pagans. They object to the way in which Paganism is often portrayed as evil. They point out that Paganism does not believe in the devil and that Pagans teach care and respect for all living things.

Most modern Pagans understand the Sacred as having male and female qualities, but refer to the Goddess as the most important way of expressing the idea that all forms of life are sacred. Above is an extract from a poem used by many modern Pagans to describe their beliefs. It is written as if the Goddess is speaking.

In this lesson you will:
- find out about the Future Forests and Chipko movements
- investigate why some people believe that trees are very important
- consider the reasons why people act to save the environment.

KEY WORDS

Global warming The process that heats up the Earth, resulting in various natural disasters

Carbon neutral A term used to describe products for which trees have been planted in order to absorb the carbon dioxide created in the production process

Deforestation Clearing an area of forest by removing the trees

HOW CAN TREES SAVE THE WORLD?

In this lesson we will look at two examples of movements that work to save the environment by looking after trees. One operates in the wealthy, developed West, but the other comes from a very poor area of the world.

ROCK STARS CARING FOR THE FUTURE

The modern music industry uses a great deal of energy and so contributes to **global warming** and climate change. Worried by this, some rock bands are taking part in a scheme called Future Forests. They pay for forests to be planted to convert the carbon dioxide created during the production of their albums into oxygen. The Foo Fighters were the first US act to participate, planting new trees in the Tensas River forest and wildlife reserve in Louisiana following the release of their album *One by One*.

The rock group The Foo Fighters were the first US band to make their album carbon neutral. Do you think this will encourage more people to buy their album?

In the same way, British band Coldplay made their best selling album *A Rush of Blood to the Head* **carbon neutral**. This means that they calculated how much carbon dioxide was created by the production and distribution of the album, for instance carbon dioxide is created by the fuel used to produce the electricity and to transport the CDs. They then worked out how many trees it would take to soak up the carbon dioxide in their lifetime. As a result, they planted 10,000 mango trees in Karnataka, India. The trees also provide fruit for the local people and for fair trade. It is possible for anyone to go to the Future Forests website and contribute.

THINK ABOUT IT!

1. Most of the wealthy celebrities who contribute to Future Forests are not religious. What do you think are their reasons for doing this? What ethical concerns does their action show?

● 'HUG THE TREES!'

In 1974, a group of women and children living in Uttar Pradesh in India, a state extending up to the Himalayas, risked their lives to save the trees around their village. Their courage and determination began a movement that has become an inspiration for those trying to protect the environment.

Many of the forests in their region were being destroyed. Big companies needed the wood for fuel and paid local people to cut down the trees. As a result of this **deforestation**, there were several landslides and floods in the area because there were no longer enough trees to stop the flow of water after the heavy rains.

When the women of a small village saw men approaching the trees nearby, they ran into the forest and held on to the trees, putting themselves between the trees and the men's axes. Their leader was a woman called Gaura Devi. When one of the men produced a gun, she said, 'This forest nurtures us like a mother; you will only be able to use your axes on it if you shoot me first.'

Eventually, the men left and the trees were saved. News of this brave act spread and people throughout north India joined what became known as 'the Chipko Movement'. 'Chipko' comes from a word that means to 'hug' or 'embrace'. Villagers clung to the trees to stop them being axed. As Hindus, they believed that the soul, a part of God, is present in trees, as in all other life forms. Some of the leaders of the Chipko Movement were also influenced by the teachings of the great Hindu leader, Mahatma Gandhi, particularly his teaching about ahimsa (non-violence) (see pages 24–7).

🎧 **As part of the Chipko Movement in India, Hindu women and children embraced trees to save them from being destroyed. Do you think that the actions of individuals can have an impact on the environment?**

THINK ABOUT IT!

2. The women of the Chipko Movement took great risks in order to protect their trees. Why do you think they were prepared to do this? Give as many reasons as you can.

3. In what ways were the women putting beliefs about ahimsa into practice? Look back at pages 24–5 if you need a reminder of what ahimsa is.

4. Use the information in this lesson and any other relevant knowledge or research to create the homepage of a website designed to encourage people to care for forests and plant more trees. Try to convince them and use as many reasons as you can. Think about what ideas and images you would use and what links you would want to make.

In this lesson you will:
- examine the evidence for the need to act in order to protect the environment
- evaluate the arguments for taking steps to change our behaviour
- reflect upon the importance of taking responsibility for your actions.

KEY WORDS

Biodegrade The process of being broken down naturally, without producing harmful waste

Interfaith dialogue Discussions and work carried out between different faiths

Did you know that if everyone in the world were as wasteful as we are in Britain, we would need eight worlds just to keep going?

- Each person in the UK uses about six trees' worth of paper a year.
- People in the UK waste a lot of water. The recommended basic water requirement per person per day is 50 litres – though people can get by with 30. The average British citizen uses 200 litres a day, the average American 500 litres. Meanwhile, in the African country of Mali, the average person has to manage with just 8 litres and in Gambia, only 4.5 litres.

It may seem that the problems facing the planet are so huge that nothing we can do as individuals will make any difference.

HOW CAN WE SAVE THE WORLD?

So, what can we do? It would seem that people living in the wealthier parts of the world need to:

- use less energy
- create less carbon dioxide
- use fewer chemicals
- make less waste
- use less water.

It could be argued that the only way in which such a transformation will happen is if the world's big companies and powerful governments join together to change their ways.

In the UK, we use 15 million plastic bottles every day and even though they take hundreds of years to biodegrade, we only recycle about 4 per cent.

● HOW ARE RELIGIONS WORKING TOGETHER?

The religions of the world have shown that it is important to work together in order to care for the environment. In September 1986, the Worldwide Fund for Nature celebrated its twenty-fifth anniversary by inviting leaders of the Buddhist, Christian, Hindu, Jewish and Islamic faiths to meet in the Italian town of Assisi. This **interfaith dialogue** ended with each religion giving a 'Declaration of Nature', which explained why their beliefs required them to respect the natural world. Later, in 1995, another interfaith meeting took place at Windsor in Britain where nine major religions took part and repeated their commitments to conservation and protecting the environment. In July 2004, the Parliament of the World's Religions met in Barcelona, Spain. One of the important debates was about how to ensure that everyone in the world could have access to safe water.

● OVER TO YOU!

Have you heard the phrase 'think globally, act locally'? What do you think this might mean?

There are many ways in which small and simple acts that we can all do make a very big impact. For example, according to the Energy Saving Trust, if every home in Britain replaced just three of its light bulbs with energy-efficient ones, it would save enough energy to power all the streetlights in the country.

Here are just a few suggestions of what we as individuals could do to make a difference:

- use public transport or cycle whenever possible
- re-use everything you can, for example envelopes, carrier bags, etc.
- take all your cardboard, glass, textiles and plastics to be recycled
- use energy-efficient light bulbs
- leave unplugged anything you are not using (do not leave on 'standby')
- only fill the kettle to the level you need when you boil water
- take showers rather than baths
- do not leave the tap running while you clean your teeth
- only use natural or environmentally friendly products in the home
- use recycled paper whenever possible (for example cards, notepads, kitchen paper, toilet rolls)
- stop using aerosols
- buy organic food whenever possible
- plant a tree or pay to have one dedicated to you.

At the 2004 Parliament of the World's Religions, nearly 8000 members of different religious communities met. They discussed ways in which they could work together to address global problems.

THINK ABOUT IT!

1. Which faith traditions can you recognize from this group of worshippers?

2. What do you notice about the different ways in which the people are praying?

3. Look at the list of suggestions opposite. Decide which you would be prepared to do and explain why. Are there any that you would not be prepared to do? Give the reasons for your decision.

4. Using the information you have gained through this chapter, decide which of these actions are the most important for helping the environment and say why.

5. Is there anything missing from this list that you could do?

WHAT THE TASK IS ALL ABOUT:

1. Write a speech for the Parliament of the World's Religions to persuade them that they should promote a united effort across different religions to provide greater care for the environment. You will be writing to convince the listener that there are many different reasons why we should take responsibility for the planet and that it is possible for everybody to help out.

2. Would you be convinced by the speech you have written? If so, what might you do to help take care of the environment? If not, what would it take to persuade you that this is an important issue for everyone?

WHAT YOU NEED TO DO TO COMPLETE THE TASK:

- You will need to include a selection of different religious beliefs and refer to the work of religious and non-religious groups.
- You should start by introducing key information about the environment that you have learned about in this chapter.
- One way to persuade the listener that it is important to act upon the information you are presenting is to refer to religious teachings.
- Your speech could end with an explanation of what other groups are already doing and what else the listener could do to help.

HINTS AND TIPS

Remember that you are trying to convince the Parliament of World's Religions that they should promote positive actions toward the environment. It will be important to refer to key religious texts and teachings, but you could also draw attention to the work of non-religious people and groups as good examples.

To achieve	You will need to
Level 3	Refer to at least two different beliefs and use them in a way that persuades the listener to think about the environment. Show what influences you own attitudes and actions.
Level 4	Choose at least two different beliefs and use them in a way that persuades the listener to think about the environment. Refer to the work of at least one religious or non-religious group. Describe what inspires and influences you to take action.
Level 5	Choose at least two different beliefs and use them in a way that persuades the listener to think about the environment. Refer to the work of at least one religious or non-religious group and explain how that work links up with the beliefs you have mentioned. Explain what inspires and influences you to take action.
Level 6	Use examples from a variety of beliefs in a way that persuades the listener to think about the environment. Show how, and explain why, the work of religious and non-religious groups sets an example for the way the listener should care for the environment. Show insight into your own views and consider the challenges posed by religion in today's world.

GLOSSARY

Absolution God's forgiveness passed on by a priest

Ahimsa Non-violence, respect for life

Anglican A Christian denomination led by the Bishop of Canterbury whose origins and traditions are linked to the Church of England

Ashram An Indian word meaning 'spiritual community'

Atman The Hindu belief in the soul, which is part of every living being

Baptism A Protestant Christian denomination who believe in adult baptism

Biodegrade The process of being broken down naturally, without producing harmful waste

Brahman Eternal spirit which is different from temporary matter. It is the source of life in all living things and in the universe

Buddha Title given to Siddhartha Gautama which means the 'Awakened or Enlightened One'

Carbon neutral A term used to describe products for which trees have been planted in order to absorb the carbon dioxide created in the production process

Castes Sub-groups of people categorised according to the social group in which they are born (also known as Jatis)

Charity Voluntarily providing help, often financial, for people in need

Church Building where Christians worship or the whole community of Christians

Civilians People who are not in the armed forces

Compassion Sympathy for people in need

Concentration camp Prison camp used in times of war to contain political and religious prisoners

Congregation Collection of people who worship in church

Conscientious objectors People who refuse to fight in a war due to moral or religious reasons

Creation The belief that the Earth was deliberately created by God or gods

Crusades War between Christians and Muslims (11th–13th centuries)

Dalai Lama Title of the Buddhist leader which means 'Great Ocean'

Deforestation Clearing an area of forest by removing the trees

Denomination A branch of Christianity

Developing countries Countries who are developing their economies and often experience great hardship

Dhammapada A Buddhist Holy Book

Discrimination To act on the basis of prejudice

Dominion Control over or responsibility for the Earth

Dukkha dissatisfaction with life. Buddhists believe this can lead to suffering

Ecological Study of the relationships between living beings and their environments, often used to describe practices which help the environment

Ecology Study of the way in which different factors work together to make life possible

Eco-systems A system formed by the ways in which living beings fit into their physical environment

Eightfold Path Buddhist teaching on the Middle Way which helps Buddhists to attain Nirvana

Emergency aid Help given to people or countries in a crisis

Environment The surroundings in which a person, animal or plant lives, often taken to mean the natural world

Environmentalists People concerned with studying and protecting the environment

Eternal life Belief in living forever

Evil Absence of goodness

Exile Forcibly sent to live in a different country

Fellowship Community within a religion

Five Precepts Buddhist guidelines about behaving well

Fossil fuels Fuels such as petrol, coal or natural gas which consist of the remains of organisms preserved in rocks in the Earth's crust

Four Noble Truths Fundamental Buddhist teaching about the causes of suffering and how to remove it from our lives

Free will The idea that human beings have been created with the choice to do either good or evil

Gaia hypothesis The idea that the Earth is a living organism, and will defend itself even against human beings

Global warming The process that heats up the Earth, resulting in various natural disasters

Gurdwara A Sikh place of worship

Hadith Sayings and traditions of Muhammad

Halal An action or thing that is permitted in Islam and food that is prepared in accordance with Islamic law

Haram An action or thing that is forbidden in Islam

Heaven Spiritual home of God

Hell Spiritual home of the Devil

Holocaust Large scale destruction, used in connection with the persecution of the Jews and other groups by the Nazis in the 1930's and 1940's

Holy war A war justified by religious reasons and fought on behalf of God or the religious community

Idols Models or images of God used in worship

Imam A leader of prayer in Islam

Indigenous The original or native inhabitants of a place

Industrialized The term used to describe a country or area which has developed many companies and factories

Inspired Feeling or help given by God, a sign of divine influence

Interdependence The idea that all forms of life depend upon each other

Interfaith dialogue Discussions and work carried out between different faiths

Jatis Sub-groups within a varna made up of numerous families who follow the same occupation (also known as castes)

Justice The principle that everyone has the right to be treated fairly

Just war Theory about when it is morally acceptable to fight a war

Karma A teaching which states that all actions will influence future lives

Khalsa The Sikh community, literally meaning 'the community of the pure'

Langar Kitchen and dining hall in a gurdwara and the food served

LEDCs Less economically developed countries where most people are very poor and struggle to survive

Liberation theology The idea that God wants all people to enjoy freedom, especially the poor whose freedoms are often limited

Long-term aid Money or other help given to a person, community or country to help overcome a long-term problem

Magga the path to release from suffering

Mara Personification of evil in Buddhism

MEDCs More economically developed countries who are wealthy, such as the UK and the USA

Methodists A Christian denomination founded by John Wesley, an 18th century religious leader

Middle Way The Buddhist Eightfold Path which creates a balance between the extremes of pain, self-denial, pleasure and self-indulgence

Moksha Freedom from the cycle of life, death and re-birth. Union with Brahman

Monasteries Places where monks and nuns live

Monotheistic Belief that there is only one God

Mosque Building where Muslims worship

Murtis Images of God used by Hindus in worship

Natural suffering Pain and suffering caused by nature

Nazi Member of the political party led by Adolf Hitler during WW2

Ozone layer The layer of gas that protects the Earth from the sun's harmful rays

Pacifists People who promote peace not war and who refuse to fight in a war or commit acts of violence due to religious or moral beliefs

Pagan Follower of a religion, based on ancient traditions, which teaches that nature is sacred

Paradise A place of perfection, life with Allah when Muslims die

Pentacostal A group of Christians who focus on praising God in worship

Persecute To bully people often due to prejudice

Pollution Harmful waste materials released into the environment

Poverty Being poor and having very few or no possessions

Praise To express positive feelings for God

Prayers Communications with God

Prejudice Believing some people are inferior or superior without even knowing them

Priest Leader of worship, especially in Christianity

Prophets People in Judaism who spoke for God and passed on his message to others

Quakers Christian group, otherwise known as the Religious Society of Friends, which was established by George Fox in the 17th century and which advocates pacifism

Racism The belief that some races are superior to others

Reservations Areas where Native Americans were forced to live after they had been conquered by the white settlers, often situated in harsh land which was difficult to live in

Roman Catholic A Christian denomination led by the Pope

Sacrifices Offerings to God

Salah One of the 5 pillars instructing Muslims to pray to Allah five times a day

Satan 'Adversary', a personification of the powers of evil

Scapegoating To blame things that go wrong on a particular person or group

Segregation Dividing people along racial, sexual or religious lines

Sewa Sikh requirement to help others

Shahadah Islamic declaration of faith in Allah

Stereotyping A generalised and simplistic mental idea of a group which is usually negative

Stewardship Looking after something so it can be passed on to the next generation

Submission Giving into the will of God or another person

Tanha Buddhist idea of craving or desire

Terrorism Using violent and illegal means to fight for a cause

Transubstantiation Belief that bread and wine actually turn into Jesus' body and blood

Tyranny Extreme government or ruler imposing their will on people

Ultimate questions Important questions that religion tries to answer

Untouchables People who are seen as the lowest in the Hindu caste system

Varnas Four classes or groups that make up traditional Indian society

Vegans People who only eat fruit, vegetables and grain, no meat, fish or dairy produce

Vicarious Experiencing something on behalf of someone else e.g. suffering

War Legal fighting either to attack or defend a country

Wealth Riches and possessions

Worship Expression of feelings towards God

Wudu Muslim practice of washing before prayer

Zakah Islamic practice of giving 2.5 per cent of savings to those in need

INDEX